	FOREWORD	
	THANKYOU	
	INTRODUCTION	8
	PART ONE	9
1	GROUNDED	10
2	FLYING!	15
3	A BIG SECRET	19
4	SAFE	22
5	ROYAL TIMEKEEPERS	25
6	PICK UP A PENGUIN	28
7	BEARS AND THINGS	32
	PART TWO	38
8	POP'S NEW JOB	39
9	MORE	43
10	CLEAN	46
11	YELLOW BUS	50
12	EVERYTHING	54
13	WAR AND PEACE	58
14	A TRICK BUT NO TREAT	62
15	QUESTIONS AND ANSWERS	PART 1	65
16	QUESTIONS AND ANSWERS	PART 2	69
17	QUESTIONS AND ANSWERS	PART 3	73

18	EXACTLY	77
19	GONE FISHING	80
20	PORTUGAL VIA SMETHWICK	83
21	OBRIGADO	87
22	LITTLE BLUE BAGS	91
23	TWO WITNESSES	95
24	A YELLOW DOOR TO GO WITH THE YELLOW BUS	99
25	THE GOOD, THE BAD AND THE MIRACLE	103
26	FIVE CROWNS	107
27	THINGS THAT COME TO LIGHT	111
28	A HORSEBOX FOR THE GOSPEL	115
29	A BIG LESSON FROM A LITTLE MAN	119
30	OH LORD, WON'T YOU BUY ME A MERCEDES BENZ?	122
31	OCEANS OF LOVE	127
32	SOMEWHERE IN SIBERIA	130
33	OUT OF THE MUD	135
34	WAKE UP	141
35	SPECIAL DELIVERY	143
36	IT'S NOT WHAT YOU KNOW, IT'S WHO YOU KNOW	147
37	LAYLA THE BRAVE	151
38	DISCIPLES	156
39	SERVANTS OF JESUS	159
40	WELLIES, SLIPPERS, PEN AND OTHER THINGS	163
41	YOU'VE BEEN FRAMED	166
42	BY ANY MEANS	170
43	THE CROWD FOR CHRIST	174
44	LABOURERS LABOURING	177
45	NOTHING FORGOTTEN	183

46	IT'S NOT TEA-TIME YET!	*185*
47	HIDDEN TALENTS	*189*
48	SUPPPLY AND DEMAND	*193*
49	JUST A TOOTHBRUSH	*197*
50	JUST SAY "YES"	*201*
51	WHAT'S NEXT?	*206*
52	EXTRA, EXTRA, READ ALL ABOUT IT...	*209*

FOREWORD

FOREWORD

In the 1960's there was well-known song entitled "Trains and Boats and Planes", I often thought that if the writer had known Dave and Penny Orange it would have been called "Trains and Boats and Planes and Trucks"! These were the modes of transportation (and others) that they used to outwork the calling on their lives of being adventurers, pioneer Evangelists, risk takers for Jesus. For the past 40 plus years they have remained faithful to that call

I first met Dave and Penny with their young family around 1982 when they were leading the Leamington Spa Christian Fellowship, I was immediately impacted by their love for Jesus and passion for evangelism. A couple of years later I invited them to join us at Devonshire Road Christian Fellowship in Liverpool, as I felt being a larger church we could support them in their calling. To my absolute delight they agreed to move. It was around this time that "All For Jesus Missions" was born with the simple goal of preaching the gospel wherever the door opened; and the doors did open both in the UK and the nations, for tent evangelism, missions and service.

In Dave and Penny (and their family) God found a couple whose hearts were after Him, with passion, love and commitment. They were, and are "All For Jesus", the mission's name was simply a statement of their own hearts commitment to their Saviour.

The following pages tell some of the stories of their adventures for Jesus, where they travelled the world by trains, boats, planes and a BIG truck to some of the remotest places to share the good news of salvation through Jesus. I first read many of these in a weekly email that came from Dave entitled "Pop's Stories", written for his grandchildren, (Maybe we should all be writing our own stories to pass on to the next generation telling of God's faithfulness!). These are true stories of adventure, risk, faith, extraordinary encounters, miracles and above all Gods amazing faithfulness and commitment to those who risk all for Jesus. These stories are being added to; even as I am writing this, Dave has just returned from another adventure for Jesus to Eastern Europe. Having had these astonishing experiences, one trait that has always remained part of them is humility, a result of walking close to Jesus.

It is an amazing joy and privilege to call Dave and Penny friends. They are unique and authentic in every area of their calling. My prayer for you as you read this collection of stories is that you too will be challenged, encouraged and more determined to give "all for Jesus" as I have been.

Len Grates
1.11.2024

THANK YOU

To Jim Hamilton for his faithfulness and patience in doing what I thought was impossible, by taking these stories and making them into a book. To Lynda Cheung, Andrew Muir and Sue Lonergan all of whom turned my writing into decent English. To Josh Catchpole for his youth and graphic design skills who brought it all together.

To South Town Church, Leamington, for standing with us in the battle. For all our five children who never complained, frequently finding strangers at our breakfast table; Dad away again; Being dragged around Europe, sleeping on the side of the road in various vehicles and waking up to the sound of yet another foreign language. And above all my wife Penny (Nana) who, as all who know us well will testify, has the patience of a saint and is the world's leading expert in deciphering my writing. And yet, despite all of this, still loves me. Amazing!

INTRODUCTION

Although far from perfect, these little stories are nonetheless my stories. They are stories of what I have seen and heard of God and what He can do even through someone like me. Those in Part 1 were written for my grandchildren, but grown ups are allowed to read them too! In part 2 I just kept on going, they are for anyone young or old, I hope you will be able to see beyond the stories to the One who is the joy of all who love Him.

My hope and prayer is that you will be able to see beyond the stories to the One who is the joy of all who love Him.

"Let me not sink to be a clod; Make me Thy fuel, oh Flame of God."
- Amy Carmichael

Dave (Pops)

PART ONE

1
GROUNDED

PELICAN BY MILLIE

"A wonderful bird is the Pelican; its beak can hold more than its belly can."

Pops was looking forward to the arrival of the pelicans; his dad (your great grandfather) had told him the little poem about pelicans and their enormous beaks and Pops wanted to know if it was true.

They arrived in big crates covered with sacking, about thirty of them, looking a bit worse for wear but doing their best not to show it - like posh ladies arriving at the Prince's ball but with their best dresses crumpled up, mud on their shoes and their makeup all smudged.

"Right, get the garden shears, David!"

"Garden shears? What do we want with garden shears?" Pops thought.

The Boss had already lifted the first pelican out of its crate, with one hand holding its body against his and with the other hand stretching its loose wing wide open.

"Now cut the primary feathers of the wing, David."

"What?"

"Don't worry, it doesn't hurt, it's just like cutting your fingernails. The primary feathers are the large feathers at the end of the wings and without them the birds can't fly. We just do it on one wing."

So, chop, chop, chop, off came the big feathers. When each pelican was clipped, we released them into their enclosure. They had a big pond for a swim, a shelter and plenty of room to waddle around.

In the days and weeks following their first nail clip, whenever he had a few minutes to spare, Pops would go to see how the pelicans were doing. They always looked a bit sad, a bit frustrated and a bit angry. Pops thought, "These pelicans look like I feel. They should be flying high over the fields, but they can't even lift themselves off the ground."

When Pops left school, he had no idea what he wanted to do, he just knew he had to work outside, if possible with animals, and so when his dad said he knew of a job being advertised for a zoo keeper he jumped at it. The zoo was over twelve miles away and his only transport was his Tourist Raleigh bike, red and cream it was. It had got him to school for five years through rain and shine, and now his trusty bike was going to take him to work. It didn't matter to him that everyone said it was a stupid job and such a long way to go there and back - he was going to work with all different kinds of wonderful animals and birds and that was good enough for Pops.

At first it was great to see and handle so many different animals but, as time passed, Pops sensed that the animals were only half living; they were in cages or fenced enclosures or, like the pelicans, their wings had been clipped. The zoo and its cages seemed to be a mirror of what was going on inside of Pops, always being angry, always annoyed with something or somebody, he wanted to tell people how he felt about things but was too shy and embarrassed to say anything. The boss said Pops had a big chip on his shoulder. He didn't know what that meant but he knew it wasn't a compliment. The animals, Pops realised, were not the only ones in cages.

His friends the pelicans looked like pelicans and waddled like pelicans but they couldn't do what pelicans were made to do - fly! But you know what happens to fingernails? (That is, of course, if you don't bite them, ugh!) Yes, they start growing again, just like the pelicans' feathers did. Bit by bit, day after day, they grew longer and longer.

"Remember to keep those wings clipped," the Boss would call out before he got into his big car. Most of his time was spent in the city doing important business, so he didn't have much time to look at everything that was happening at the zoo.

Well, the feathers never got clipped. Pops was not very good at obeying grownups, either at school or now at work; it got him into a lot of trouble! But he wanted to see his pelican friends do what they should be doing: he wanted them to fly!

Monday morning started like most mornings, only this morning the wind was blowing hard, straight into his face, making it difficult to cycle at his usual speed, even with his three gears! He used to get very angry with the wind, shouting at it, telling it how stupid it was! It would never seem to blow behind him, helping him to go faster, but always in Pops's face - the wind was just one more thing he hated!

Pops got to the zoo hot and sweaty and still angry with the stupid wind. But soon he had made up the first buckets of feed and was on his way pushing the trolley to the first set of pens, which always took Pops past the pelicans.

Pops stopped and stared: "Of course, the wind!" He forgot he had been angry with the wind, for the pelicans were loving it. They were all standing on the highest point in their enclosure, facing right into the wind and flapping their big wings, feathers completely grown again.

"This is it; this is the day they are going to fly," Pops said to himself. "Go on, go on, flap harder!"

Pops found himself not only shouting at them to fly but his arms were going up and down too and he was jumping on the spot. "Watch, do this!" he shouted. He was a very strange boy and not a very good zookeeper!

Then it happened - one had lifted off the ground, only half a metre at first, then higher and higher, then another and another, then suddenly they were all flying. Pops thought to himself, "Surely they can't get over the fence, can they?"

But they could, and over the fence they flew, over the rest of the zoo and out into the countryside. What a sight, great big birds doing what they were made to do. They were flying, they were free. As Pops watched them disappear his heart began to sink: "Who is going to make me fly, who can make me free?"

The Boss was not very happy; it took two days to capture them all again. He threatened Pops with the sack and Pops didn't blame him; it was his job to keep the animals in, not help them all to go free.

"If ever I get free," Pops thought, "nobody is ever going to catch me, but who can make me free? Who can make me into the person I want to be?"

When the answer came, it came as a great surprise!

2
FLYING!

PELICAN BY JOSH

All the time, while Pops was clipping wings, chasing pelicans and pulling elephants' tails at the zoo, somebody was praying for him.

"You are joking! Church? You're going to church! You'll never get me there!" was Pops's answer when his friend finally plucked up the courage to tell him where he went on a Sunday evening and Pops decided he would be going in the opposite direction.

But as the weeks passed Pops's friend seemed to be getting happier. Pops on the other hand was getting unhappier, and he couldn't understand why. He was doing all the things that he thought should make a young man happy and they had nothing to do with going to church.

Pops secretly hoped his friend would ask him again. Well, he turned out to be a good friend and he did ask him again, and this time Pops went too.

Pops thought they were all a bit posh. They were all going to grammar schools and getting loads of A-levels ready for university. Pops had never even got a Z-level. But they were very friendly towards him, which made a nice change. Even though they kept talking about a man called Jesus who loved him so much He died for him, Pops kept going back and started to enjoy himself, except the bit when the man at the front started talking about love and joy and peace, which Pops didn't know much about, also about uncleanness, anger and swearing, which he did know a lot about.

Pops realised that if he was going to be part of these new friends he would have to try and be like them, at least on the outside. Stopping swearing would be a good start. He tried, but failed - even in their meetings Pops heard himself swearing and he hated it.

Back at the zoo, Pops was looking after six dingoes, beautiful Australian wild dogs, larger than a fox but smaller than a wolf, whose coats were the colour of Wetherell's toffees.

Pops could tell that, like him, they were not happy; they were always angry and looked frustrated and hated being caged up. They walked up and down their cage, never resting, never seeming to be peaceful, neither with one another nor with themselves. Sometimes when he was in their cage, they would stand for a few seconds and stare at Pops, maybe contemplating whether they could attack him. At such times, Pops would shout at them and they would back away.

One Saturday afternoon they all escaped and when he got to work on Monday morning, he was told they had killed and savaged the neighbouring farmer's sheep, and they had all been shot. The Boss had tried calling them back with their favourite food, but it was useless. "They were wild animals," Boss said, and being caged up had made them twice wild. They could not change their behaviour, and Pops realised neither could he.

One Sunday evening at the youth meeting, someone was talking again about Jesus the Son of God who loved us and died for us. Just like those dingoes, Pops had had enough. He started shouting "Why should He? I never asked Him to love me, I never asked him to die for me." Pops went dingo crazy. He started throwing the chairs about, running around the hall pulling down the brand-new velvet curtains from the windows, and fighting anybody who came near him.

Some of the young men eventually overpowered Pops and dragged him to the door. The pastor had heard all the noise and came into the hall and stood right in front of Pops. He had white hair, and Pop thought he looked very old.

With his hands in his pockets he said, "David, you are banned from this church. Don't come back until you have changed." They stared at each other.

Pops thought, "He's old, I can easily handle him," but as Pops looked, he knew that there was something inside of this old man that was stronger and better than what was in him. Pops walked past him and out of the door.

"That's it!" Pops thought, "this Christian thing is not for me; like those dingoes, I can never change."

The next two months were horrible. He tried to go out and have fun at night but came home just as angry as ever, and sometimes worse. At the zoo it was as if the animals were all saying to him, "You're in a cage, just like us."

Late one night in his bedroom, Pops decided he had to do something. For the first time in his life he got on his knees by his bed and cried out, "God of the Christians, if you can do anything with me, please do it!" As soon as the words came out of his mouth, something heavy and dark lifted from him and a lightness and happiness just came rushing in. He knew that the God of Jesus had forgiven him, and he was free.

When Sunday came, he put on his best clothes (because that's what he thought you had to do) and went to church. The pastor was standing at the door, his hands still in his pockets.

Pops said, "Can I come back? I have changed." The pastor said, "I know, I can see! Of course - come on in." Pops was flying.

3
A BIG SECRET

ELEPHANT BY FAYE

A long time ago, when Pops left school, he got a job looking after the animals in a zoo. There were all kinds of animals: sea lions that barked; lazy zebras that would never take off their PJs; ostriches that looked like upside-down broom sticks; vultures that always looked at Pops as if he was their lunch, and many more.

This story, though, is about a baby elephant.

Pop's job was to feed him five times a day with warm milk and rice, which Pops put in a milk bottle and then pushed into his mouth. They became good friends. As soon as Pops came into the stable, he would run up to Pops and reach out his little trunk like an arm and shake Pop's hand - but Pops had to be careful because, although he was small, the baby elephant could still very easily push Pops over.

Pops's boss said he must feed him bananas as well as milk and rice, and he must peel them before he gave them to him. But Pops discovered that if he put a banana on the floor, Gordon - (it was 1966, England had just won the World Cup and Gordon Banks, England's Goalkeeper, was Pops's hero, so Pops decided to call the baby elephant Gordon) - Gordon learned that if he squashed the end of the banana just right, then it would shoot out of its skin - well, sometimes it did! This became one of Pops's and Gordon's secrets - it had to be a secret because for every banana that he shot out, there would be lots that became a squashy mess on the floor and Pops's boss wouldn't like that very much. But their best secret of all was that Pops learned that if he pulled Gordon's tail he would always walk forward. And one day this little secret became very important!

Pops's boss was being paid by a comedian to take an elephant down to London airport so she could be filmed pulling an elephant through passport control, just like you pull a suitcase. (I know, stupid, hey?)

The big truck pulled up one Saturday morning to take Gordon and Pops down to London, but Gordon would not get into his box on the truck. Pops's boss, the driver and the driver's mate were all pushing Gordon as hard as they could, but he would not budge. The boss didn't ask Pops to help because bosses always know best. But if they couldn't get Gordon in soon, they were going to be too late, so the boss grudgingly asked if he could help.

"Sure," he said. Pops went up to Gordon and pretended to whisper something to him, at the same time giving a little pull on his tail, and like magic Gordon went straight into his box. All the men were amazed.

"How did he do that?" they said. Pops just smiled.

They got down to London airport where the famous comedian was waiting with the cameras and film crew.

"Oh, David, we will take it from here," the boss said - but of course Gordon wouldn't move.

"Can I help?" Pops asked.

"No, you're too scruffy for the television," said the boss.

"He'll be fine," said the comedian. "Although he looks scruffy it seems the elephant likes him; it will make good TV."

So, pretending to whisper in Gordon's ear and at the same time, without anybody noticing, he pulled Gordon's tail. Off the elephant went, and scruffy Pops went through London airport on the telly.

"What a remarkable young man", they said; "a boy who can talk to elephants!" - because nobody knew their secret - just Gordon and Pops.

Now, as you know, Jesus made not only elephants but ostriches, vultures and all the animals, and the reason He made so many is because He wanted to show us things about Himself through them.

One of the things Pops was learning was that if he spent time with Jesus, like he spent time with Gordon, He would start showing him things about heaven and earth, about God and man, and best of all, about Himself. When he began to spend time alone with Jesus, sometimes Pops thought his heart would burst with His loveliness!

So, next time you need to take an elephant for a walk, remember Pops's secret. And if you want to know Jesus better and better, just spend more and more time with Him.

4
SAFE

CHICKEN BY JOSH & JAKE

Last week, Miss Lily Johnson (Pops's granddaughter) asked if Pops knew any stories about chickens. Well, as it happens, Pops did.

This story takes place on a big sugar cane farm in the middle of Kenya. Kenya is in the middle of Africa and right in the middle of the sugar cane farm lived a man, his wife and their five children. They were one of the happiest families Pops had ever met; they all lived in a small round hut, with walls made of mud and the roof made of dry sugar cane. The floor was made of cow muck, not soggy cow muck because that would have been disgusting, but rock hard cow muck, and Mrs Buwane would sweep the floor every day so that everything was very clean and tidy.

In the hut there was a small wooden table just big enough for Mr and Mrs Buwane and one guest to sit and eat at. The children would always sit on their small beds which were also made of cow muck and so was the guest's bed - and guess who was the guest? Yes, it was Pops! So Pops has slept in a bed made of poo!

Mr Buwane and his family used to live in a big town, where Mr Buwane was a bank manager and Mrs Buwane a teacher. One day God spoke to them and said He wanted them to leave their jobs and their nice house and go to the sugar cane farm, to preach the gospel to all the people who lived and worked on the farm. So they did exactly what God had said and I suppose that was the reason they were so happy.

Mr Buwane had invited Pops to help him preach the gospel. Every afternoon they would walk to a big clearing in the field where a wooden stage had been built. There would be lots of music, singing and dancing and everybody would gather round the stage. There were about two thousand people, workers and their children from the farm and the surrounding villages.

Every morning, if Pops wasn't visiting people, he would sit outside their hut drinking tea from Mrs Buwane's best china - a lovely baked bean can! Mrs Buwane kept chickens and while Pops was living with the family, one mother hen produced a lot of eggs and the eggs produced lots and lots of baby chicks.

One morning, there was Pops with his baked bean tin of tea watching Mother Hen clucking away happily and all the baby chicks running all over the garden looking for things to eat. One would pick at an ant, another would be trying to catch a fly and never succeeding, while others would be turning over leaves to see if there was anything worth eating underneath. It was a beautiful African morning with a pure blue sky and the sun not yet hot enough to chase the "mzungu" (a white man) into the shade of the hut.

Everything was peaceful in the farmyard: the chicks were chirping, Mother Hen was clucking, and Pops was drinking his tea. Then suddenly the hen's voice changed; she stopped her friendly clucking and now it was a loud alarm as if she were calling all her baby chicks to come back to her as quickly as their little legs could manage. From all over the yard baby chicks were running back to mum. What was the reason for the panic?

Pops looked up. There high above the farmyard was a big bird of prey ready to swoop down and take one of the little chicks home for his lunch - but he was just too late! Mother Hen had opened up her wings like a huge feathery umbrella and all her family were hiding safely under them; as she closed her wings she gathered all her children safe under her and there wasn't going to be any takeaway chicken for Mr Eagle that day!

One day as Jesus was talking to the people in the city of Jerusalem, He looked at the crowds and cried out, "Oh Jerusalem, Jerusalem, how often have I wanted to gather your children together as a hen gathers her chicks under her wings."

Jesus sees danger long before we do and calls out to His children. If we let Him, He will gather us under His wings where there is no fear but perfect love for every child, big or small, who puts their trust in Him.

5
ROYAL TIMEKEEPERS

CROWN CRANE BY JOSH

Do you ever think about how God made all the animals?

There must be thousands and thousands of them, from the tiny flea to the huge blue whale. What an imagination He must have! Who would have thought of putting a gold crown on the head of a bird with a long black neck, great big black and white wings and long grey legs? Well, He did, and we call it a crown crane - and they look beautiful.

Pops saw his first crown crane years ago while he was working at the zoo. This zoo was like a big animal supermarket; lots of different animals would be delivered in lots of different crates, then zoo owners from all over the country would come to buy what they wanted for their zoos. So, Pops got the opportunity to handle lots of different animals.

Pops remembers the first time he touched a crown crane; its head was like two fairy cakes squashed together with icing on both sides and very fine black feathers on top that felt like velvet - and then, right on top of that, a beautiful crown made of feathers that looked like very stiff golden thread.

Pops thought to himself, "Well, I wish I could see them flying in the wild." Who would have thought that one day he would?

Many years later, in Kenya, Mr Bawane told Pops that the people must leave the meeting for their homes before it got dark, because there were no streetlamps, no buses, no cars and no electricity in their homes.

Well, while Pops was preaching, to his amazement two crown cranes flew over the stage and with their big wings glided over the crowds and into the bush. They had been feeding all day and now they were going back to roost for the night because they knew it would soon be dark - but Pops didn't!

Pops simply carried on preaching, but he had made a big mistake! The people had to leave to hurry home while there was still just a little light left, and Pops had not given them an opportunity to come to Jesus. Pops hadn't understood how quickly it gets dark in Kenya – it's just like when you turn the light switch off.

Pops felt very bad; he had let the people down, he had let his friend Mr Bawane down, but most of all he had let Jesus down. The next day, Pops was determined to do better.

He was pretty sure that the cranes would fly over at the same time every night and so the next evening as soon as Pops saw the cranes, he knew it was time to stop preaching and invite the people to receive the Lord Jesus. Every day was the same - his two crown cranes would fly over; he would immediately stop preaching and the people would come and give their lives to Jesus - and all before the daylight finished.

We must let the light of Jesus shine into our hearts, now, while we can say yes to all that Jesus through His Holy Spirit is saying to us. Then, like Pops's friends in Kenya, we can go on our way knowing the happiness that comes by knowing Jesus.

6
PICK UP A PENGUIN

PENGUIN BY FAYE

Back at the zoo crates were still being delivered and Pops was still being surprised by what was in them.

"Ouch!" Pops had done something that you should never do if you are receiving crates delivered to a zoo, especially when labels on the crates say, "THESE ANIMALS MAY BITE."

Although Pops had become a Christian, he still hadn't learnt to obey and take notice of..... well, notices. He had put his hand inside one of the crates and now his fingers were being pulled off by very sharp, very strong pliers - but pliers that made a lot of noise. He pulled his hand out of the crate as best he could, but the pliers would not let go. The pliers had a head attached to them and then a black and white body attached to the head and two funny looking wings attached to the body.

"Penguins, they're penguins!" Pops cried.

That seemed to satisfy the pair of pliers that was crushing Pops' hands; it let go of his fingers and dropped back into the crate where it was congratulated by the other pliers for making yet another human scream in agony.

"Well done, David, very observant," said the Boss, with a little smile on his face. "To be precise, they are Humboldt penguins. Now these penguins will probably refuse to eat and if they don't eat, they will die."

Pops was going to say something clever like, "Cor, is that right?" but he thought better of it.

"So," Boss continued, "you must force feed them once every day with fish until they recover from their journey and are willing to eat again on their own."

"How?" asked Pops, who was still trying to bring some life back into his swollen fingers.

"Easy! Just catch them one at a time, sit down, put the penguin firmly between your knees and with one hand force its beak wide open and with the other hand push the fish down its throat. Then hold its beak shut and rub its throat until you can feel the fish go down. Good, now I must be going - important things to do in the city." And with that boss was gone, leaving twenty penguins looking at Pops as if to say, "You just try it, mate!"

So, the battle began. To feed a penguin, first you have to catch a penguin. At least now Pops knew why the boss hadn't filled the penguin pool with water. Penguins can swim faster than zookeepers but zookeepers (at least, fit and handsome zookeepers!) can run faster than penguins.

By the end of the first week Pops' hands were covered in cuts and bruises and his clothes covered in bits of very smelly fish and his own blood. But gradually one by one the penguins started to feed themselves, picking up the fish that Pops threw to them, and they began to put on weight and look a lot fitter - all except one.

Pops had already noticed that there was one penguin that couldn't pick up the fish because its beak had been broken and had healed all wrong, so however hard it tried, it just could not pick up the fish from the ground. After feeding time the rest of the penguins would waddle off, probably to discuss how boring life had become now there was no human to savage. But Percy (Pops had decided to call him Percy) just stood there looking very sad and very hungry.

"Well, Percy, what are we going to do?"

Pops was now talking to a penguin! Percy half turned his head and looking at Pops with one eye, he opened his beak. There were a few fish left at the bottom of the bucket, so Pops took one out and held it out to him. Percy waddled up to Pops and took the fish out of Pops's hand. That was it - the start of a beautiful friendship.

The penguin pool soon got filled with water, so most of the fish could now be caught and eaten in the water, but whenever Percy saw Pops come through the gate, he would climb out of the water and stand beside him. Pops would feed Percy by hand, maybe asking how he was doing and if the rest of the penguins had settled in.

One day, when Pops was going back out through the gate of the penguin enclosure, Percy followed him and as Pops turned to close the gate they nearly tripped over each other.

"Would you like to see the rest of the zoo, Percy?" asked Pops.

Percy put his head to one side and looked at Pops with one eye, which in penguin language means, "Yes please." So Percy started following Pops around the zoo and Pops introduced him to all the animals, except, of course, the big sea lions because sea lions love penguins, especially for afternoon tea. But Percy knew he was always safe because he was with his friend Pops.

Because of his broken beak Percy was different from the rest of the penguins. Sometimes, Pops felt just like that, because he was different from the rest of his new Christian friends. They seemed so much better than he was, they talked more easily and knew a lot more stuff than he did. All of them were set to go off to university, and they lived in bigger houses and had gone to posher schools. Sometimes Pops felt embarrassed when he was invited round to their homes and would say something stupid, when one of their parents asked something about himself.

But as Pops learned that he could trust Jesus, just like Percy trusted Pops, he became less and less self-conscious. The broken beak didn't bother Percy - in fact, what could have been a disaster for him turned out to be the best thing that could ever have happened. Now he could walk freely around the zoo whenever he wanted to or just swim with the rest of his penguin friends, all the time knowing that Pops was always there looking out for him.

As Pops started to read the bible, he began to realise that it had taken much more than a few cuts and bruises on His hands to rescue Pops. Jesus had laid His life down for him.

Those first friends of Pops, even after fifty years, are still some of the best friends Pops has ever had although he doesn't see them much now. But Jesus has been the best friend of all. He said, "I will never leave you or forsake you," and Pops has proved that to be true over and over again!

7
BEARS AND THINGS

BEAR BY HENDRIX

Nana told Pops that he needed to write a story about bears and because Pops knew it was usually a good idea to do what Nana said, he thought he would.

"Oh, I know," said Pops, "What about a story about a bear that loves honey?"

"Don't be silly, that's been done," Nana said, giving Pops a little kiss on the cheek. Pops was beginning to like writing stories if he got kisses.

"What about a bear that travels from Peru to England?" Pops was waiting for another kiss, but he didn't get one, just one of Nana's looks which some of the naughtier children in the Orange family know all about.

"Well, what about this one?" Pops said and started telling it.

Henry was a real live lumberjack, and he lived with his family high up in the Canadian Rocky Mountains. He told Pops it sometimes took him and his crew three days driving big 4x4 trucks to get to where the trees were being cut down. Often they would see not only bears but mountain lions and loads of other wild animals too.

Henry was part of a small church that had invited Pops to preach in a little town in Canada called Fernie. Because Henry's church loved God, they were very hungry for more of Jesus, so they would eat up even the smallest things Pops could tell them, just like children on an Easter hunt eating the chocolate eggs as soon as they found them - which of course was never allowed on Nana's Easter Hunt, but somehow always happened.

"Do you want to come and see the bears?" Henry asked Pops. Pops wasn't sure what to say; he had left the zoo a long time ago and didn't really want to see any more animals in cages. Henry seemed to know what Pops was thinking.

"Don't worry, they are not in cages, they are wild," Henry said with his big Canadian smile.

"What? Wild? You mean really wild?" Pops said, trying his best to smile back with his not-so-big British smile. "Yes, please, I think I do." So it was arranged that after the last meeting they would set off.

The last meeting had finished, and Henry and Pops were driving out of town in Henry's big red pickup truck to see the bears. The road was heading into the mountains.

"This is wild country with wild bears," thought Pops and he made sure his door was firmly locked. Suddenly Henry turned off the road into what seemed to be the town's rubbish tip. (I expect it's called the recycling centre today.) He stopped the car and got out and Pops followed.

"Do you want your rifle, Henry?" Pops asked. Henry was a

lumberjack and always carried a rifle in his truck just in case.

"No, we'll be OK – look!" Henry pointed to the middle of the rubbish dump and there, hunting through the rubbish, must have been at least fifteen bears, big brown bears, smaller black bears, even one or two baby bears, all enjoying a free supper on food the humans had thrown away!

So what people thought was rubbish, the bears were loving. Henry said that every night the bears would be on the rubbish tip, eating until they were full. So, the bears, Henry's church and Pops were all being fed on food that other people thought was not worth keeping!

King David wrote, "The word of God is sweeter than honey, so taste and see that the Lord is good."

They watched until the sun disappeared behind the mountains and then left them to their meal.

The next day Pops had to leave Henry and his hungry friends to fly down to Mexico, a long way from Canada's Rocky Mountains. There he met his friend Xavier.

Xavier was quite different from Henry. Henry was a quiet, thoughtful man like his mountains and had a great big heart. Xavier was not quiet, but very loud, always joking, and when Pops was with him Pops was always the joke.

Because Pops couldn't speak Spanish, he asked Xavier to teach him a good sentence so that when he started preaching Pops could look as if he could speak the language. So, standing in front of nine hundred Mexicans, Pops proudly spoke the words Xavier had taught him. Instead of clapping and smiling and nodding their heads, they laughed and laughed. Xavier had taught Pops to say, "I have a very ugly face" instead of "It's great to be with you all today"! That was Pops's good friend Xavier!

A few days and hundreds of jokes later Xavier announced they were going to a RUBBISH tip to preach.

"Not to bears?" Pops spluttered.

Xavier stared at Pops. "Gringo, you English are strange people! Why do you want to preach to bears?" Pops said nothing, just followed Xavier to his car and they both set off for the rubbish tip.

The rubbish tip was huge, fifty times bigger than Henry's Canadian one, and all over there were shacks made out of plastic, cardboard, bits of wood and even bits of broken windows. People were actually living and working on the rubbish tip - husbands and wives bringing up their children right there on the tip.

A man came running over to them waving his arms. (It was a Mexican waving, but that was before the "Mexican wave" was invented!)

"So happy to see you, thank you for coming! I am the pastor and this is my congregation," he said.

Pops didn't know what to say, he was crying.

"Please come and meet everyone, they are so excited to meet you." So, after being hugged and kissed by fifty Mexicans plus their children, they had a church meeting. Try not to think of a church service you may go to in England - there was no building, no chairs, no hymn books, no one dressed up in robes, but heaven came down on that rubbish tip. Singing, shouting, dancing, jumping for joy.... these were the happiest people Pops had ever met.

"We have to go now," Xavier said.

"Already? We've only been here a few minutes," Pops said.

"No, we've been here three hours, Dave, and we're going to be late for the next meeting."

As they travelled back in the car, there were no Mexican jokes or English jokes; both men just wanted to remember what it was like to be in heaven.

*****

Georgi was taking Pops to meet his grandmother, who lived in a little cottage in a big forest in the middle of Estonia. One of the qualifications for being a good pastor, it seemed to Pops, was to be a mad driver. Georgi was a very good pastor! The old Dacia was bumping all over the road, covering the thousands of wildflowers with a thick layer of dust.

It took them about an hour to get from Georgi's town to his grandmother's and when they arrived, she was working in the garden that surrounded her cottage.

As soon as she saw them, she shouted, "Georgi, you shouldn't drive so fast - the dust gets everywhere! Now, come on in."

Inside was exactly what you would want a grandma's cottage to look like. Pops was going to make a joke about Little Red Riding Hood, but he thought better of it.

"You have got a lovely garden, beautiful flowers and so many vegetables. Do you have much trouble with the rabbits coming to the garden and eating your cabbages?" Pops asked, thinking it would be a nice question to ask this sweet old lady.

Georgi, with a slight grin, translated for his granny.

"Rabbits? No, not rabbits, BEARS! I chase the bears away in Jesus' name and with the help of this." And she picked up a football rattle from the little table next to her chair and with one hard swing, it went round and round above their heads - it was very loud.

"Rabbits!" she said again, looking at Pops and shaking her head, as if to say, "Silly Englishman!"

So Pops discovered a little old lady living in the middle of the forest who chased bears away with a football rattle, shouting, "In Jesus' name, go!"

Not for the first time Pops was realising that you can't learn everything about Jesus and his kingdom from a book.

PART TWO

8
POP'S NEW JOB

Most of Pops's friends had left the zoo. Gordon, the crown cranes, the pelicans and Percy the penguin - all of them had found new homes in zoos up and down the country. Pops had also left; he didn't want to clip any more wings or force food down any more throats. He was glad that he had left – but what to do now?

A man who was to become one of Pops' heroes told him, "Stand still and be quiet and you will know what to do."

Pops interrupted, "Stand still? I'm 17, how can I stand still and be quiet? I want to DO something for Jesus!"

Eddie said, "Hold on, I haven't finished. Allow God's Holy Spirit to lead you and you will know what to do."

Sometimes Pops's mouth was quicker than his brain!

Within a couple of days Pops had got a new job. John, one of his friends in the church, told him of a temporary job helping with the harvest on the farm where he worked. It was perfect and Pops started the next day.

It was brilliant, driving tractors, stacking straw bales onto trailers, and carting them away from the fields into the barns.

But the best job of all was following the combine harvester. Pops drove the tractor that pulled the special trailer that caught all the corn that spilled out of the combine. The tractor raced back to the farm, up to the tall silos and tipped the load of corn into the big pit where a special machine took it up to the top of the silo. Everyone worked flat out from early morning to late at night. Nothing was more important than getting all the harvest in before the autumn weather arrived.

It seemed to Pops that the same things were happening at church. More and more people were coming and joining the church, not just young people but people of all ages - there seemed to be an invisible combine harvester at work. Pops didn't understand how it was happening, but it was great fun. In fact, he decided he wanted to live like this forever.

Then one day without any warning the harvest on the farm was over, the last trailer-load of corn had been tipped and the last straw bale had been stacked under the big roof of the barn.

"Well, Dave, what do you think of farming?" the farmer asked Pops.

"Brilliant," Pops said, still a little shy when talking to older people.

"Well, we would like you to stay on full time."

"Oh yes please!" Pops was going to become a real farmer, driving tractors and everything.

The 'everything' came as a bit of a surprise. The farmer had just bought a new field and he wanted to take John and Pops to see it, so they jumped onto the trailer and the boss towed them with the tractor to the new field. The field followed a river for a long way and Pops couldn't quite make out where it ended.

"I like this field; this field is going to be very good for us," said the farmer. Pops felt very special that the farmer should confide in them both and wondered what job he wanted them to do. Pops hoped that it would be to plough up the field. He'd watched somebody ploughing and thought that it would be a great job to do even though he hadn't the first idea how to plough.

"Right, I am going to drive slowly up and down the field and you two will walk behind the trailer and pick up all the large stones and boulders you see and throw them in the trailer."

It took Pops and John three days to clear that field of stones. Pops had thought he was quite fit and strong but by the end of third day he could hardly walk and only just lift his knife and fork to eat his dinner, which in all his life before had never happened, as Pops liked his food.

What a difference from all the fun and excitement of the harvest! During harvest he was driving tractors all over the farmer's fields, up and down all the lanes and through the villages, but with this job he was focused on just one field and just one small piece of that field making sure that he didn't miss any stones, most of which were the size of footballs.

Pops really liked the farmer but in his heart, he couldn't help grumbling: "Look at the farmer just sitting on that tractor all day and us working like slaves under the hot sun! Who does he think he is?" Pops didn't like himself for thinking like that, which only made him feel worse.

When the job was finished and the field was clear of stones, the farmer said, "That was a very important job and it had to be done. If we'd left the stones, the plough and other machinery would keep getting smashed and broken, but now the field is clear, we can get on and plough - I'll teach you."

Pops started to think, "Could my heart be like the farmer's new field?" The farmer had bought the new field and was very pleased and excited about its future, but if he'd left the stones, then it would never produce the crops of wheat that the farmer wanted. Pops was still feeling so free and happy knowing that Jesus had forgiven him everything, but just as he and his friend walked up and down the field looking and removing anything that wasn't what the farmer wanted, so the Holy Spirit was beginning to look and remove stones from Pops's heart. Stones of grumbling, they had to go, Pops's tempers, his arguing, his swearing, and feeling sorry for himself - enough stones to fill up a lot of trailers. Some were deep down: just as Pops sometimes had to dig to release a stone, so the Holy Spirit had begun digging deep in Pops's heart.

Pops wanted more than anything to have a heart like a good field where Jesus could grow a crop and harvest it over and over again. So Pops was determined to say "Yes" every time the Holy Spirit discovered another stone that had to be removed.

9
MORE

The clouds were black, the winds were blowing hard, the rain was pouring down and Pops's feet were squelching in his wellies.

"It surely won't happen again tonight?" thought Pops, "and how can I count these silly sheep when they refuse to stand still?" That was Pops's last job before he went home, to check the sheep were OK and see if they were all there.

The farmer had taught Pops to count the sheep in fives, using his hand with his palm stretched out towards the sheep and roughly counting in groups, with his four fingers and thumb.

(You should try it sometime and if you are anything like Pops you will come up with a different total every time! A long time ago, Pops discovered that his children were a lot brainier than he is and he has a horrible feeling his grandchildren are twice as brainy as their parents - but don't tell them that because having a big brain is good but to have a big head is bad!)

Pops was getting very wet, counting very soggy sheep and thinking about what had happened the previous night. That had been a beautiful evening; the sun was setting, turning the sky red and making the clouds look like fire and Pops was so glad to be alive. Suddenly he found himself praising God for His amazing creation, and he even started to sing which didn't sound much different from the sheep's bleating! (Pops is not the best singer in the world - come to that, he's not the best counter of sheep either.)

Pops was overcome with joy. Then from somewhere deep inside his heart new words started bubbling up into his mouth and out into the autumn air. When Pops realised what was happening, he put his hand to his mouth and stopped.

"This is bad! I've been told about all this - they call it speaking in tongues and some churches don't allow it." The praising stopped and Pops hurried home; he would go and ask his friend Eddie what he thought.

Pops found Eddie with his Church of England dog collar on, working in the church. Pops was nervous and not quite sure how to start the conversation. Before he could say anything, Eddie said, "Sit down, Dave. I've just been praying and speaking in tongues."

Pops said, "How did you know that's what I wanted to ask you about?"

"I didn't but I have just been praying, so go home and see what the Bible says."

So Pops did and there it was in black and white: they spoke in tongues all over the place.

Well, here was Pops again in his soggy wellies, counting his soggy sheep in a very soggy field; it was still God's creation but a very soggy creation!

And now inside Pops's heart something was happening again; springs of liquid love started bursting up. The love of God, the love for God, the sheer joy of His love overflowed him. No hymn Pops could remember or words he could say could possibly express what he wanted to say - but then new words, a whole new language, flowed up and out into the rain and Pops knew this wasn't wrong, this was the Lord. This was the Holy Spirit helping him to worship his marvellous and wonderful God.

Years later Pops discovered the story of a French lady called Madame Guyon who had been locked up in a horrible prison called the Bastille four hundred years ago in Paris. That was a whole lot worse than Pops' soggy field! And in her prison she sang this:

"I love my God but with no love of mine

For I have none to give

I love Thee Lord, but all the love is Thine"

- Madam Guyon

10
CLEAN

The time had come to ask Nana's dad for permission to marry his daughter. It took most of Saturday afternoon and innumerable cups of tea. (Cups with saucers were always a problem for Pops - if you spilled tea in the saucer, were you supposed to pour it back in the cup or, when nobody was looking, slurp it from the saucer? Pops decided not to do either, but then noticed spots of tea dripping on his jeans.)

"Oh well, here goes," he thought.

"Mr Shilling, Penny and I would like to get married – please!" There, Pops had said it. Just one problem - Mr Shilling had fallen asleep. Nana had to wake him up and Pops had to go through the agony all over again.

Pops's mum and dad would be much easier. So, the next day, after Sunday tea, he said, "Mum and Dad, we are going to get married!"

"Oh, David!" Pop's mum looked surprised and said, "That's a big commitment for any girl, who to? Who would want to marry you?"

Nana was standing next to Pops. "Me!" she said, "I want to marry Dave."

"Oh, good then," replied his mum. His dad looked at them both, filled his pipe, lit it, and said, "Good for you, congratulations!"

And that was it…. on September 4th, 1971 they were married. Yes, that's right, more than 50 years ago!

Four years after the wedding, Pops, with zoos and farms behind him, was now working on building sites as a hod-carrier and enjoying the life that God had so graciously given him. The Bible had changed from being a closed, stuffy book and was now the most exciting thing that Pops had ever read. There were huge bits of it he didn't understand, but the bits that he did made his heart leap and very often reduced him to tears.

But as he read, a conviction started to grow and take hold of him. He knew he needed to be clean. He became desperate to be clean like the Bible said, in his 'inward parts,' in his thoughts, and in his heart: 'Blessed are the pure in heart.' He knew he was forgiven and each time he asked Jesus, He would forgive him again (which was a lot of forgiveness). But he felt there had to be something better. He just wanted to be clean, so clean that his heart would be a holy place for Jesus to live in. He realised he wanted to live like the disciples did after Pentecost.

He said to Nana, "I want a New Testament life."

"What do you mean?"

Pops said, "I'm not sure, I just know that my life and the life I read about in the New Testament are at odds with each other and it's driving me mad."

Late one evening Pops got a phone call from two ladies

whom he knew slightly through their children. Their car had broken down travelling back from a Christian meeting. Pops borrowed a car and went out to fetch them home.

On the journey back they were both bubbling with excitement about the meetings they were going to and what they were hearing.

"God's so much bigger than we thought, Dave, and He wants to do greater things in us and through us than we ever thought possible!" said Dulcie. "Would you like to hear a tape of one of the meetings?" asked Marg.

"Ok, thanks," Pops said, a little sceptical. "I'll listen to it sometime."

In fact, Pops played it that night while Nana was sleeping. The next day Pops decided he must get to that meeting. He asked his two new friends if he could go with them and of course they said 'Yes.'

Pops can't remember a word anyone said, but he knew God wanted to make him completely clean, and could do so - in fact, He could give him a new heart. All the way through Pops kept saying, "Yes, Lord, that's what I want, yes, Lord, yes, Lord." By the end of the meeting Pops knew God had done something that He thought was impossible: He had taken Pops's old sinful heart away and given him a pure new one, one that knew God and loved Him and everyone and everything.

Pops knew that the next day, the next week, the next month would be the real test of what God had done. It was one thing to feel the love of God in a Christian meeting, but the proof of the pudding would be on the building sites, in the streets of the town and in the secret places of his heart, where no one can see except Jesus. In the past Pops had been to rock concerts and remembered the euphoria while the concert was on, but the second it had finished so had the euphoria, and down to earth you came.

But the wonderful thing Pops was experiencing was nothing to do with man's work. This was God's mighty Spirit taking the power of sin away forever and washing him clean right down to his boots and all he could do was praise Him.

Charles Wesley wrote:

O for a heart to praise my God,

A heart from sin set free!

A heart that always feels Thy blood,

So freely spilt for me!

11
YELLOW BUS

It was going to be an exciting day. Nana, Pops and their friend Mike were going to drive down to London in Mike's car to buy an ambulance. Not a "der, der" ambulance but a much bigger type, the kind that transported people back and forth from different hospitals to their homes, so that instead of having stretchers it had twenty proper seats.

Pops's friend Evelyn had started a youth club called "Into the Future" around the same time the film "Back to the Future" was showing at the cinemas. Because Evelyn was the best youth club leader ever, "Into the Future" was getting very popular in the town and so a bus was urgently needed to get all the children to the club on time.

Nana was taking Uncle Dan and Aunty Ruth to Quack Quack Grandma's for the day. (Uncle Dan at a very early age, as all the Oranges will testify, knew everything about everything and so when Grandma first took Daniel to the park to feed the ducks, all ducks were renamed Quack Quacks and Grandma renamed Quack Quack Grandma forever!)

"Don't forget to ask the Lord how much money we must give for the bus!" Pops shouted to Nana.

"Yes, dear, I know, I can remember what you told me five

minutes ago," Nana replied. She said something to the children which Pops couldn't hear, making them both giggle and they disappeared round the corner.

After Nana had safely deposited Daniel and Ruth at Quack Quack Grandma's she joined Pops. As soon as they had all jumped into Mike's car and were on their way, Pops asked Nana, "Well what did the Lord say?"

"We are to give £600 and not a penny more," she said.

"YES! That's exactly what the Lord said to me too."

"What do you mean?" said Mike. "I think we'll have to spend a lot more than that! You know we collected nearly a thousand pounds."

"But we will have to obey God - if He says £600 then £600 is what it will be," said Pops.

"Ok, that seems reasonable," Mike said, putting his foot down on the accelerator of his SX2000, making a very pleasing noise from the engine. It was always good fun driving with Mike.

An hour and a half later they were in the office with the two brothers who owned the second-hand bus business and Nana had managed to find a place to sit that wasn't covered with oily rags or fish and chip papers. Mike, Nana and Pops had taken the ambulance for a test drive and knew it would be absolutely perfect for the job it had to do. The bigger of the two brothers slapped his hand down on his very old desk which looked as if it would collapse with the weight of his hand.

"£900 and it's yours!" he said.

"We can only give you £600," responded Pops.

"£600?" shouted the big brother. "You know it's worth £1000, don't you? I can't give it to you for any less than £850."

So, the bargaining continued, Pops insisting it should be no more than £600 and the big brother gradually bringing the price down until it fell to £650.

"Look!" Pops said," God told us this morning you would sell that bus for £600 and we can't give you a penny more."

"God told you, did He? Did he also tell you that if I give you that bus for £600 you would be robbing us?"

"Sorry," Pops said, "£600 it has to be."

The big brother looked at his little brother who just shook his head.

"Please, if I let you have it for £600 it will be an embarrassment for us. Everybody who gets to know will say the brothers gave in to the God squad! We'll be a laughing stock - what about £601? Then we can all go away happy."

Pops knew it was far more important to do what God had said than to drive home with the perfect bus but knowing he had disobeyed God. He got up from the secondhand car seat he was sitting on, shook the brother's hand and said, "Sorry but we can't do that."

Pops, Nana and Mike walked out of the office down the yard towards Mike's car.

"We have nearly £1000," said Mike. "We can't go back without the bus, it's just perfect."

Pops, with a big grin on his face, said "Before we drive away, he'll come running down and agree the price."

And sure enough, before Mike had time to start the engine, big brother came running down to Mike's car!

"OK, OK, you win - £600 it is and not a penny more."

With the money that was left over, the church had the bus painted bright yellow and put in new seats and a new engine. Then they had "Red and yellow, black and white, all are precious in His sight" written in big letters on one side and "Jesus Loves You" on the other.

The Jesus bus became well known all over the town; whether you loved it or hated it, no one could ignore it. Pops loved driving the big yellow Jesus bus but what he enjoyed most of all was discovering what the Bible says - that "God is not a man that He should lie." Because of that fact, Pops knew that whatever was going to happen into the future, he could trust God.

12
EVERYTHING

Something had happened to Nana; she was all shiny and twinkling.

It was Saturday morning and Nana and Pops had been invited to a special Full Gospel Businessmen's meeting in a posh hotel in Leamington. Nana, as usual, was giving Daniel and Ruth their breakfast and making sure everything was ready for when Aunty Julie and Val came round to babysit for them.

"God's done something wonderful, Dave," Nana said while she cleared away the breakfast things and then made sure Pops looked at least half presentable for a posh meeting.

"Yes, I can see He has."

Nana had always been the most beautiful girl Pops had ever seen but this morning there was something more, something he couldn't find the right words for.

"What's happened?" asked Pops.

"We must go now or we will be late. I'll tell you later, come on," replied Nana, leading Pops out of the door. The Manor Hotel was only a quick fifteen-minute walk from their house in Wise Terrace.

"No time to talk, Dave, or we'll be late," Nana said, urging Pops to hurry up.

When they got there, the function room was already filling up with local Christians and their friends whom they had invited to hear what God had done in different people's lives. Some were standing drinking coffee and some already sitting down at the round tables that had been set around the whole of the room, complete with tablecloths, vases of flowers, tea and coffee pots, plates and cutlery.

"Bit posh, isn't it, Pen?"

"Don't worry about that! It looks like they're going to give us a good breakfast," Nana replied.

"Ah, not so bad then, let's sit down."

This was the first time Nana and Pops had been invited to a FGBM meeting. Most of the people knew who Nana and Pops were, and although the leaders had been a little sceptical of Pops's and Nana's new church in their house, they were very loving and gave them both a warm welcome.

After a very good breakfast the meeting started with a few songs and then a couple of Christians were asked to go up to the front and tell something of their experience of Christianity. After they had finished and the clapping had stopped, there were a few seconds of silence.

Suddenly Nana stood up and said, "I want to say something, please."

Pops looked at her and nearly fell off his chair. This was not like Penny - she hated speaking in public, and in the few times Pops had dared to ask her to speak in an open-air meeting she had made her feelings well known afterwards to Pops. But here she was now, already at the front of the meeting and thanking the chairman for kindly allowing her to speak - not that he could have done much to prevent her.

One or two people had started to leave but when they saw that Penny Orange was going to speak, they all quickly got back in their chairs. The people all became very quiet: this was that sweet Penny Orange, what on earth was she going to say?

She started, "Some of you may know that Dave my husband has started to travel to different countries, sometimes away for a month or more. When we are saying goodbye, I always try to put on a brave face for him and for the children, but as soon as I can I run up to the bedroom and cry to God to help me. I'm scared something may happen to him or the children and also, I hate him being away, even though he can be a bit of a pain sometimes."

(Laughter and a few nodding heads from the tables.)

"But God did something wonderful for me last night. I have been reading the biography of Rees Howells and yesterday I got to the place where the Lord showed him that he needed to give everything over to Him and that God would show him specific things over the next twenty-four hours. Through the next day the Lord brought to his mind those things and by the end of the day he was able to give everything to Him. Immediately I knew I had to do the same. I thought I had given all my life over to Jesus some while back, but the Lord made it very clear that the two things I was keeping back were Dave and the children. Could I really give them over to God and totally trust Him for them? I know it sounds silly, because of course God can do a better job than I can, but does God love Dave and my children more than I do?

"It was a real struggle but by the end of the day I did it. 'Lord,' I said, 'they are yours,' and then such joy and peace flooded my heart. I have never known such love from God pour into my heart and I love Jesus more than ever. I just had to come and tell you what God had done for me. Thank you for listening."

Since then, for at least thirty years Pops has spent up to six months every year away from Nana and the children and although it has sometimes been lonely and sometimes very difficult, she has always had the certainty of God's unfailing love and care for her and her family.

Paul the Apostle wrote this to his friends in Rome:

"I beseech you therefore, brethren, by the mercies of God, that you present yours bodies as a living sacrifice, holy, acceptable to God."

13
WAR AND PEACE

A week to go and Pops would be off again, this time to America, Canada, and Mexico; he was already getting nervous.

"If only I could drive or go by boat or even row across," was what he thought every time he had to fly - he hated it. He hated everything about it. Saying goodbye to Pen and the kids, queueing (he still hates queueing), wandering up and down the duty-free shops just waiting for the command to board.... He reckons terminals are one of the loneliest places on the earth. Then there's the actual flying, with sweaty hands, stomach churning upside down every time there is the slightest bit of turbulence. And then, when it's smooth, wondering if the engines are still working. And, of course, all the stuff the hostess puts in front of you to eat, juggling plastic knives and forks, hoping your drink doesn't tip up over the chef's so called special dessert - or is it the meat course? - has Pops got them the wrong way round?

Then Pops would be feeling guilty because he was wishing he'd said no to the invitations; he'd be asking himself if God had really called him to preach the gospel and wishing that he was looking out of the window and seeing those beautiful patchwork fields that say welcome home to Heathrow.

"Now fasten your seat belts, at last we are about to land."

Then bump, bump, we've made it! Hallelujah, all is forgotten! Until the next time.

For two weeks Pops sees God doing wonderful things in people's lives and asks for forgiveness for ever doubting Jesus and His mighty gospel, but then all of a sudden he's alone again in Chicago airport, waiting for his flight to Calgary, and here come the sweaty hands and all the fear comes flooding back.

Pops thinks of Penny who loves flying.

"What's not to like?" she says, "A nice comfy seat, time to relax, a nice read, someone serving me drinks and meals that I haven't had to cook, even time to write my Christmas cards and maybe do a bit of knitting."

(This was in the olden times when sharp knitting needles were allowed and there was a bit more leg room!)

"Right, that's it, this is ridiculous!" Pops said to himself this time, and then to the Lord. "Lord, I have three hours before my flight, I'm preaching about the love and power of God and I'm scared stiff of flying. I'm a hypocrite! I am locking myself into this toilet and I'm not coming out until you set me free from this uncontrollable fear, please Lord."

And in that toilet God did set Pops free, and off he went with a skip and a jump to board his flight.

On that flight Pops found himself in the middle of a Roman Catholic convention, with maybe four or five dozen priests and nuns on their way to a conference in Calgary. Pops had a priest on one side and a nun on the other and they started talking about religion. Pops said he didn't know much about religion, but he did know Jesus.

"In that case you must come back to mother church," they said. Pops thanked them for their kind invitation and asked them who the head of their church was.

"The Pope, of course," they replied.

"Oh, the head of my church is Jesus so maybe you would like to come back to mine," Pops replied with a bit of a cheeky smile. Pops was a very young man back then and hopefully over the years he has become a little more gracious. Hopefully.

The seat belt sign came on and the flight was on its final descent into Calgary airport. The pilot apologised in advance for the bumpy descent, explaining that because the airport was so close to the Rocky Mountains the flights had to descend slightly faster than usual and there would be some turbulence. There was a lot of turbulence, and everyone suddenly became very quiet. All around Pops prayer beads came out and heads began to bow, but Pops was as happy as anything and started sharing with his new friends what God had done for him in the airport - and with no interruptions.

In two weeks' time he was off again, this time flying from Spokane to Guadalajara, courtesy of Mexican Airways. The pilot thought it would be nice to give the passengers a free trip around Mount St Helens which had just erupted! One or two passengers seemed to enjoy the view, but most were looking for their sick bags.

"That was good, would you like to go around again?" the pilot asked, and so having put ten Pesos in the slot around they all went again.

"British Airways was never as good fun as this," thought Pops, but then sadly the pilot headed south, and all became calm.... until, that is, somewhere over Mexico the plane hit a huge electrical storm. Looking out of the window Pops was reminded of the films he had seen of the desert battle of El Alamein during the Second World War; everywhere there were huge explosions of light and thunder, while Pops was worshipping the God of all creation. Outside there was war, but inside his heart there was perfect peace.

Now people were being sick, baggage was falling out of the lockers, people were being lifted off their seats, even with their seatbelts on. Over the screams, the pilot informed everyone that he was going to make an emergency landing.

On the third attempt the plane touched the landing strip and finally came to a stop. The passengers were then informed that the pilot would take off again as soon as possible because the airport where they had landed was not an international one and therefore no one could dis-embark. Immediately there was a stampede for the exits and people were banging on the doors, pleading to get out. Pops suggested to a hostess that it might help if the pilot said they would only take off again when the storm had passed. However, the flight deck remained silent until two hours later when the weather had calmed down; then the seat belt signs flashed, and the pilot told everyone it was now safe to continue their journey.

The old proverb says 'the proof of the pudding is in the eating,' and God had proved to Pops that His peace that passes all understanding certainly guards and keeps a man's heart, even a heart of a 'scaredy-pants' like Pops.

14
A TRICK BUT NO TREAT
(WRITTEN FOR HALLOWEEN)

"Lord, this can't be right, I'm a preacher and a minister of your wonderful gospel and here I am still having these nightmares! How can I talk about the love that casts out all fears when these nightmares are making me scared stiff?"

That was Pops praying; he had been preaching for three or four years and very occasionally he would have the same nightmare, finding himself struggling to wake up while shouting the name of Jesus and then waking up in a cold sweat.

While he was praying God reminded him of something he did when he was still a very young Christian.

He and his friend had decided it would be good fun to play a trick on two girls.

The plan was to walk the girls home one evening, but to make sure that at midnight they would all be standing outside the church. Pop's friend, a great storyteller, would tell them the story of a ghost that appeared on top of the church tower once a year at midnight. At the same time, Pops, with a big white bed sheet tucked up his jumper, would climb up the outside of the tower with the help of a big drainpipe conveniently tucked into the corner and hidden from the pavement below.

At midnight his friend was going to casually ask the girls what day it was and after they replied, he would say, "Oh, would you believe it - that's the same day that the ghost is supposed to appear!"

When the church clock struck twelve, Pops walked around the top of the tower with his sheet over his head. His friend and the two girls looked up and his friend asked, "Can you see anything?" and then the two girls fainted – they were out cold.

By the time Pops had climbed back down, the girls had recovered and were sitting in his friend's house, drinking hot tea and being comforted by his mum. Pops thought it best to make his escape, but it was too late; although his friend hadn't confessed who the amateur ghost was, to Eddie it was obvious. Eddie was waiting for him; Pops had never seen him so angry and he was made to apologise to everyone, especially to the two girls.

"This is no way for a Christian to behave, David," Eddie said. Pops was ashamed and once again resolved to do better. After Eddie had prayed for the two girls they were seen safely home.

Now years later the Lord had shown Pops the cause of the nightmares and his foolishness. Pops was very ashamed and with tears asked God to forgive him. God in His incredible grace and love did forgive him and Pops, now seventy, has never been troubled with nightmares since. He admits that although he was a teenager (yes, even Pops was a teenager once upon a time) his conscience was being pricked as he climbed up the drainpipe - but being the stubborn boy he was, unlike that little man Zacchaeus that Pops loved to preach about later on, he didn't have the sense to climb back down.

You can find the story of Pops's friend Zacchaeus in the New Testament, Luke chapter 19

15
QUESTIONS AND ANSWERS | PART 1

DANGER: HEALTH WARNING! If you try and figure out which story goes where in sequence, you may end up with a very bad headache. Pops tried and Nana got the headache!

Pops was speaking at a conference in Minnesota and one afternoon the students from the local Bible School asked if there could be a Question-and-Answer session, after the compulsory game of soft ball of course. Pops hoped the questions were going to be about football (real football i.e. soccer) or rugby or even cricket but they turned out to be serious questions; he'd wanted to tell them that soft ball was like the game that English girls played called rounders, but alas, the moment had passed.

Out of all the questions that were asked there was only one that Pops remembered later.

"What will happen to those people who have never heard of Jesus?"

Pops felt he had been hit by a cricket ball (harder than a soft ball of course) and the room became very quiet.

After some time, his answer was, "I don't know, but we must go and tell them."

That was the last conference Pops ever preached at. Later that evening he said to himself, "If I wasn't the speaker here, then these incredible people could get somebody far more able and far better qualified than me and they would do a much better job. From now on I am going to speak to the lost!"

When Pops arrived home, the first thing he said to Nana (well, nearly the first thing) was, "We must do the work of an evangelist."

"How?" asked Nana.

"I don't know yet," Pops replied.

So the church prayed and decided that Pops would go and see an evangelist that they had heard good things about. Pops came back very excited.

"He's brilliant, just the man for us."

So it was arranged that the evangelist would come down to Leamington with his big tent for two weeks in August. The church knew exactly where they would put the tent, in the part of the town where all the real "Punks" hung out, complete with chains, braces, boots, and parrots on top of their heads. This was going to be great, thought Pops, a church full of punks - he couldn't wait!

Everything was arranged and posters, flyers, invitations to all the other churches to come and help. Then two weeks before the great day the evangelist telephoned Pops to say that he was very sorry, but it was going to be impossible for him to come.

"Well, can we still have your tent?" Pops asked.

"Sorry, that also has to be somewhere else, but don't worry,

I'm sure something will turn up."

"That's all right for you to say, mate," thought Pops. With some difficulty he put the phone down rather than throw it out of the window - but realising his heart was not quite as pure, loving and forgiving as he thought it was, then he repented. Pops still had a lot to learn about the ways of God. Although he didn't know it, this was going to be the means of pushing Pops out of his "comfortable nest" so he could learn to trust God and fly without any ropes attached. Scary!

When Pops told the church the news, they all said, "You will have to be the evangelist, Dave."

"But I'm not an evang..."

"You are now," they all shouted. When the laughing finally stopped, the next question was: where do we get a marquee from?

The answer, of course, was the same as always: "We need to pray", so all Friday, Saturday and Sunday the church prayed.

Pops was now a self-employed hod carrier and labourer and for the last couple of weeks he had been working for a friend who was a builder.

By the way, please don't ask Pops what a hod carrier is as he will only have to climb up a ladder with a load of bricks to show he can still do it - and he can't!

On Monday morning, Pop's first job was to carry bags of cement out of the store, but he was finding it difficult because of a load of huge bags and poles that had appeared over the weekend.

"What are those big bags and all those poles?" Pops asked his friend Jim. "I've never seen them before, they weren't here last week."

"Oh, they came on Saturday - it's a big marquee I'm storing for a friend who wants to sell it. Why, do you want to buy it?"

"YES!" said Pops immediately. "How much is it?"

"£2000 and it's yours".

So, even while the church was praying, God was answering. All they needed now was £2000!

16
QUESTIONS AND ANSWERS | PART 2

Where are we going to get £2000 from?

It might as well have been two million pounds, it seemed impossible.

But Pops and his friends were realising "impossible" was a good place to start, so again Friday, Saturday and Sunday became "knee drill" days (that's an old Salvation Army expression, meaning they were praying).

By Sunday evening the church believed God had answered, even though only about two hundred pounds had come in - but then during the week Pops received though the post a cheque for one thousand pounds!

It was from a church in Birmingham who were holding tent meetings in Victoria Park, Smethwick, which (as every geography student knows, so Pops says) is "the centre of the universe." Pops was excited to know that there was another church that was just as crazy, happy and full of love as the one he belonged to.

During that week the rest of the money they needed came in bit by bit; sometimes a pound, sometimes twenty-five pounds, sometimes by post or just dropped through the letter box.

Pops and the church were now the proud owners of a 300-seat marquee - and there it was, a great big, tangled heap in the middle of the park. There were huge sheets of canvas, all different shapes and sizes, ropes of all types and colours, an assortment of metal stakes, some very long poles, some short square poles... In fact, everything that was needed to build a marquee was there - except the owner's manual!

It was 8 o'clock Saturday morning and at 9 o'clock the leaders from the other churches in Leamington would arrive to help put the marquee up.

At 10 o'clock the tangled heap looked even more tangled. Pops was feeling very embarrassed; he had been lovingly told by mature Christian leaders that maybe he was not experienced enough or his theology was not as it ought to be... The tangled heap just confirmed their suspicions, but they were good men and did their best to help and encourage.

By 12 o'clock there had still been no progress, apart from a few more knots appearing in ropes and one or two bruised shins where poles had decided that gravity was a reality and sky hooks were not!

Then Pops had a brainwave: he said to everyone, "I know Jesus was a carpenter and not a tent maker, but I bet if we asked Him, He would show us what to do."

So everyone bowed their heads. Pops wasn't sure if they were bowing their heads in prayer or in sympathy.

Some bright spark said, "Maybe we could ask St Paul at the same time because he was a tent maker!" There was some laughter but Pops prayed anyway.

"Lord Jesus, we haven't a clue what we are doing - please help us."

Then Nana arrived with bags of chips for the workers, and prayer and chip butties did the trick. Everything became clear and the big jumble started to look like a beautiful marquee. By 7.30pm when the first people were arriving for the meeting, the last few chairs were being arranged and the PA was being tested.

Nana and her friends were on the stage and started singing. To Pops's surprise, the marquee was quickly filling up with Christians from all over Leamington, including a lady pushing her son in a wheelchair, who came right down the centre of the meeting and sat on the front row.

Pops suddenly felt very hot and sweaty; he wished he hadn't worn a tie, he wished he hadn't bought a marquee, he wished he was still driving a tractor on his own in a field - but he was wearing a tie (for the last time), the marquee was bought and he was standing on the stage facing a mother and her son who had come expecting a miracle.

Nana and their singing group had finished their songs and sat down. The next thing to do was for Pops to preach, because that's what he had seen done in other missions - first some singing, then one or two Christians would give their stories about how they had come to Christ, then the preacher would preach and then invite people to receive Christ.

But this dear mother looked at Pops and Pops looked at her, and before he knew properly what was happening, Pops had got down from the stage and was standing in front of the boy. Nana thought, "Oh no, what's he going to do now?"

"Do you want to be healed?" Pops asked the young boy.

"Yes," he replied, so Pops held the boy's hands and pulled him out of the wheelchair. The boy stood up and then walked up and down; because it all took place so quickly, hardly anybody knew what had happened and the meeting just carried on, including some unexpected entertainment from a local lad riding his motorbike at the back of the tent!

Nana, who was sitting right behind the young boy, couldn't believe it, and Pops couldn't believe it, but there he was - walking! It might have appeared to others that Pops was full of faith, but the very opposite was true. As he had stood on the stage, looking at the boy in his wheelchair, he had felt that the mother would be pushing her son out of the marquee the same way they had come in, with nothing changed. He had felt no faith at all, just panic to get it over and done with as quickly as possible and then to advertise: "For Sale - One 300-seater marquee, hardly used!"

But God is a lot bigger than Pops, and Pops is very glad He is. If our chief scientist (Aunty Rachel) is right (and she usually is) that the universe is still expanding, then Pops reckons that it's growing only because there is still not enough room to express the unsearchable grace and mercies of God.

17
QUESTIONS AND ANSWERS | PART 3

Nana Rules OK

Where were the punks and skinheads? Every night the tent was being filled with Christians but none of them was wearing chains or nose rings, there were no bovver boots or braces and not a single parrot on the top of anybody's head - it was getting serious.

Reports were coming back to Pops from different churches that people were getting really blessed.

"How?" asked Pops.

"The Holy Spirit," said his friends. "Don't worry, Dave, it hasn't got very much to do with you." (Pops loved his friends and his friends loved Pops.)

At the end of the first week the church asked God to bring the punks to the tent and God was pleased to answer abundantly!

They came but not just in the tent. On top of the tent was a favourite place for the young people to listen to the gospel. They soon discovered that the tent roof made a great slide - and why use a public toilet when there are three holes placed right at the top of the marquee for their convenience, plus a pole to keep them steady?

But maybe the best fun was when they discovered the orchard next to the park. The apples were just the right size to throw but still very hard, perfect ammunition. In they would charge, pockets full of ammo and all directed at anyone who dared to stand on the stage.

If you have ever wondered why the ladies in the Salvation Army wore those funny hats, it was because when the Army started, it wasn't just apples thrown at them, but rocks, stones and bricks. Salvation Army soldiers were killed in the line of duty on the streets of England, so the hats were reinforced to give them some protection. However, in our marquee there were no fatalities, just a few bruises.

While Nana and her friends were singing, Pops and one or two men would stand in front of the singers and try catching the apples but still some got through the defences. So on the third evening Pops distributed his secret weapon: dustbin lids - brilliant! Now hardly any missiles were getting through. However, the only problem now was the noise the apples were making banging into the metal lids. But everyone was having great fun - Nana and her friends were singing as loudly as they could, the punks and skinheads were sliding down the marquee roof, the occasional beer bottle was being thrown into the congregation, fire extinguishers were being let off and barrages of crab apples were continually being sent to the front as if the whole marquee community were preparing for a harvest thanksgiving service!

Then suddenly, above all the din, Nana shouted and everything stopped and there was quiet. (You Orange children and grandchildren will understand!)

"You stupid boys, don't you know you could run out of this tent, across the road and be hit by a bus and die, and then you will be standing before God's judgement seat and He will ask 'why didn't you listen to My Gospel when you had the chance?' "

For a few seconds, punks' eyes and preacher's eyes were all looking at a very beautiful, very pregnant Nana. Then every swear word that Pops had ever heard was being shouted at Nana and with one accord they turned and stampeded out of the tent, laughing and jeering.

Pops thought he had better carry things on and started to preach but something was happening at the back of the tent. People who had been brave enough to remain were now turning to see what was going on outside.

Slowly, sometimes on their own, sometimes two or three together, the punks started to come back into the tent. No one was shouting or swearing, no apples were being thrown, just dropped quietly onto the ground, and like a well-behaved Sunday School class they all sat down on the chairs.

"What's happened?" asked Pops.

"Just what the lady said," replied one of them, maybe a girl, as they usually turn out to be the bravest!

"We did all run out and ran over the road but we didn't see the bus coming and one of our mates went right under it - but then he just popped out the other side and all he's got is a couple of bruises, so we reckon it must be your God trying to tell us something, so I suppose you'd better tell us!"

Pops just looked at those kids hidden behind their braces

and their chains and knew at that moment that God loved these kids with everything He was.

Pops can't remember exactly what he told them, but it was probably something like this:

"Jesus told a story about a boy who took everything his father gave him, then turned his back on his dad and wasted everything he had been given. When he had nothing left and nowhere else to go, he at last looked at himself and said, 'I've been stupid, I am going back to my dad and I am going to beg for his forgiveness.'

"His dad had never stopped looking out for him and when he saw his son coming back home, he ran to him and again gave him everything he had."

Pops said, "Jesus told that story, and it is Jesus himself who has taken the blame and guilt for all that stupidity and wastefulness by hanging and dying on the cross. The moment any person, whether punk, preacher, policeman or pensioner, believes this, they will be forgiven and receive eternal life."

The punks seemed to understand, and some of them decided they wanted to know more about this Jesus. Pops also decided that he too wanted to know more about this Jesus and to tell the world what he knew.

.

18
EXACTLY

By midnight most of the marquee and equipment were safe in Pops's friend's bakery. The last of the PA equipment had been recovered from various parts of the park where some of the guests in the marque had invented one last game, a variation on the Easter Egg Hunt - but instead of chocolate eggs, there were loudspeakers, microphone stands and the last of the fire extinguishers (after they had been emptied, making them easier to carry - very thoughtful!).

Next stop, Victoria Park, Smethwick - but how to get the marquee and all the equipment there?

The yellow bus was great but 4ft x5ft bags of canvas and 21ft poles could never fit through the doors. Pops tried, but just thinking positively is sometimes not enough - it only gives you a hernia and a big headache! A trailer had to be the answer.

Pops needed information about trailers. So Pops asked Nana very nicely to get on to it straight away! Telephones, paper and pens were never Pops' friends: a comment from one of his school reports said "This may have been a good essay, Orange, but I could not read a word of it!"

There was no internet back in the old days, only telephones and the Royal Mail. Soon Pops's little study floor was covered in shiny pictures of trailers and lots of technical information.

"Pen, give me a hand," shouted Pops. (If Nana and Pops are laid next to each other in graves, Pops's gravestone will say, "Pen, give me a hand" and Nana's will say, "Yes, dear"!)

So Nana gave Pops a hand sorting everything out.

"Right," said Pops, "This is what we need."

Nana knew exactly what Pops needed, but love covers a multitude of sins, so she quietly resumed the hundred and one things she had to do before it was time to collect the kids from school.

"A trailer 12ft long and 8ft wide with twin bogey wheels and a capacity of three and a half tons costs £3000. Piece of cake - I'll tell the prayer meeting tonight." Nana had already left for school and Pops, not for the first time, was talking to himself.

Pops had conveniently forgotten that the church was still recovering from: two weeks of flying missiles; putting up marquees; dismantling them in the middle of the night; cleaning canvasses, chairs and various pieces of equipment that had been splattered with foam from emptied fire extinguishers; following up people who had become interested in the gospel; and apologising to different church leaders about their equipment they had borrowed that might have gained a few scratches.

"But praise God, brother! People seem to have been added to the church!"

"This is what we need - a trailer," Pops told everyone, "12ft long, 8ft wide, twin bogey wheels and able to carry three and half tons, £3000 - lets pray."

When Sue arrived home from the prayer meeting, her husband Mike asked, "How did the meeting go?"

"That man is impossible!" Sue had always been very discerning. "We prayed for a trailer but not just any kind of trailer, oh no! It has to be exactly 12ft long, 8ft wide, twin bogeys (whatever that means) and a capacity of three and half tons - and only £3000. Penny is a saint!"

When Sue arrived at work the next morning, there was a notice on the notice board that read:

For Tender

1 Trailer 12ft long 8ft wide, twin bogeys, capacity three and half tons

Sue asked her boss, "My church needs a trailer; how much do you want for it?"

"If it's for your church, just offer £50 and you will get it. The trailer isn't needed anymore, it was made specially to move plant around the factory which is why it has an unusual spec."

So, Pops got his trailer, Nana got a big hug, but God got the glory! And the church grew a little more in faith and in understanding of how very serious Jesus is about evangelism.

19
GONE FISHING

One Saturday, when Pops was still at school, his dad took him to a fishing competition. It was held on the river Stour, just south of Stratford upon Avon where Pops was born.

They had to start very early in the morning because great granddad's Austin 7 got very annoyed if he tried to make it go any faster than 30 miles an hour. It would start wobbling its front wheels, the little windscreen wiper (just one) would start jumping up and down and lots of very grey smoke would appear from under the bonnet, but Pops thought it just did that to show his dad that it could produce just as much smoke as his dad's pipe. His dad's pipe always won!

There were about twenty men in the competition; each one had a "peg" on the riverbank, and they couldn't fish anywhere else while the competition was in progress. Pops was the youngest in the competition and his peg was next to the most experienced man in the competition; he even had little badges that he had won fishing pinned to his hat.

The whistle blew for the start of the competition and Pops put his favourite bait, two pinkie maggots, on a No 14 hook - lovely!

"I'll show Badge Man next to me how to catch fish - thinks he's the best, does he?" said Pops to his box of maggots. (Pops was a very strange boy!) "I'll cast out as far as I can and then Mr Badge Man will see what an expert caster I am."

It was a very hot day. Pops was catching nothing but Badge Man on the next peg seemed to be catching fish far too often for Pops's liking. Pops was still showing off with his long casts, but his neighbour was doing the opposite, just short casts every time and making his float pop up just beside the lily pads that separated him and Pops. Eventually Pops realised what was happening. Because it was a hot day the fish were sheltering in the shade of the lily pads and not even Pop's juicy pinkies could entice them out of the cool shade.

The whistle blew for the end of the competition and the judges came down the line weighing the catches. Pops got his catch out, a couple of manky tiddlers, which hardly moved the scales. Next was Badge Man - plop, plop, plop, plop, loads of fish making the scales jump as if it had hiccups. Of course, Badge Man won.

"Why didn't you follow what I was doing and put your float next to your side of the lilies?" Badge Man asked Pops.

But Pops just shrugged and said "Dunno" and walked away before he did something with the pinkie maggots and Badge Man's hat. Pops just couldn't talk to grownups, especially when they were right, and he was wrong. He knew what was happening with the fish but because of his stupid pride he could not bring himself to change what he was doing, and because of that pride he had no fish and had lost the competition – and Pops hated losing.

Many years after Pops's conversation with the maggots, he had never forgotten his stubbornness and the empty net. Now, as a Christian, Pops knew if he was going to be a fisherman for Jesus and catch men for Him, he would have to do it the Jesus way. The disciples fished all night and caught nothing but as soon as they heard the Lord's voice and cast their nets on the right side of the boat their nets were full.

Pops was determined to turn his back on his foolish pride and stubbornness and discover the secrets that Jesus had taught his disciples and the many Christians down through history who had become expert fishers of men. He read about George Fox, George Whitfield, John Wesley, Charles Finney, D. L. Moody, Hudson Taylor and many others, and he realised they had one thing in common: they had discovered the secret of prayer. And once they had discovered it, they prayed and prayed and prayed, and as they prayed God changed them so that they started living and fishing the Jesus way.

20
PORTUGAL VIA SMETHWICK

Sometimes Pops was asked to help repair brick kilns in a brick factory in a town called Kenilworth not far from where Nana and Pops lived. Pops and his friend Jim would always do the work at night when most of the people who worked at the factory had gone home.

There must have been about sixteen kilns, all built next to each other in a very big circle. The clay bricks felt a bit like Play-Doh and were carefully packed into one of the kilns. When the doors were shut, the fire which travelled slowly from kiln to kiln would be let into the one that had just been filled with the wet bricks. It was left until the fire had done its job and all the bricks had become rock hard, then the kiln would be emptied and the bricks loaded onto lorries and transported to different building sites.

Even when a kiln had no fire in it, it was still very hot. Pops's job was to take out any of the old fire bricks that were part of the kiln's roof but had been damaged over time by the heat. He had to put new ones in with a special fire cement. He would race in, put three or four bricks into place, and then race out as quickly as he could before he became a hard-baked brick too! When Pops described to Nana what the job was like, Pops told her he was grateful that he had learned to jump out of things that became very hot!

Pops had read stories about different parts of the world where God had poured out His Spirit, just like the fire in the brick kilns. Somewhere in the factory there was always at least one kiln filled with clay being made into bricks by a red-hot fire, and somewhere in the world God was doing the same thing in His church. He was pouring out His love and power into people and making them into a living building where Jesus would carry on doing all His incredible works.

Pops asked God if he could meet people who had been in that special fire that the books called revival, so God sent him to Portugal where he was to meet Brazilians! and this is how He did it.

There was an old missionary called Harvey, who Pops first met in the big tent in Smethwick. He really should have a whole book written about him, as he was a man who would do anything and go anywhere for Jesus, a real brick.

Harvey asked Pops, well, kind of told Pops, that he must take his tent and have a mission in Portugal, so Pops said "Yes." Pops had decided some time ago always to say "Yes" unless the Holy Spirit said "No." Pops discovered that was a great way to live, although sometimes it could be a bit scary.

So, Pops, Nana, their four children and a small team set off with lots of tins of baked beans, corned beef and stewing steak and butter beans (Pops's favourite), camping stove and gas, sleeping bags, suitcases, a double buggy and a potty! They went on a five-day journey to North Portugal - thirty-five years ago, there were no motorways in Spain or Portugal and mobile phones did not exist!

The team had only enough money to drive down to Ramsgate to catch "The Sally Line" ferry for France. What the team didn't know was that Pops had no money for the ferry tickets or fuel for the rest of the journey through France and Spain. Pops had told God about that little problem and God had said, "Trust me don't tell anyone." The only other person to know was Nana - Nana always knew everything about everything, especially about how many pennies Pops had left in his pockets, and she knew all the pockets were empty.

The yellow bus reached the ferry terminal, and all Pops could do was to trust God and join the queue for the tickets. The queue moved slowly forward until there were only two vehicles left in front of the yellow bus before Pops needed to buy the tickets with money he hadn't got.

Just then there was a tap on Pops's window. Pops wound the window down and a man asked, "What's all this then?"

The yellow bus was very, very yellow and had "Jesus loves you" in big written red letters on both sides. Pops explained, then the man said, "Well, you are going to need this" and he gave Pops an envelope. Inside it was enough money for the tickets for the team, the yellow bus, and the trailer! The man then he got back in his car and drove away. Pops calmly (another miracle) paid for the tickets and drove onto the ferry.

One of the team had promised to phone her dad to let him know how things were going, which she did when they arrived in Calais. She came back with the news of how her dad had put a credit card in her luggage for emergencies, but now he told her it must be used to buy diesel for the rest of the journey. If Pops had told the team earlier that there was no money for the tickets, she would have volunteered to pay, but this way God was able to show Pops and Nana that even though they were just two baked bricks they could absolutely trust God who will never let them down.

If you still feel like a piece of Play-Doh that just gets squashed by things around you but want to be used in God's building, then ask Him to put you in His fire – but, be careful, because it can get very hot!

PS Pops was going to tell you about God's Brazilian bricks that the Lord had sent to Portugal and how Pops taught them to play football! But that will have to wait until next week.

21
OBRIGADO

The yellow bus had finally reached Portugal. They were minus one of the team, Linda, who had developed pleurisy, but Pops had found a wonderful missionary family in Spain where he was able to leave her until she was well enough to join the team in Portugal. And because she was born again in South Town Christian Fellowship in Leamington, Linda was a "toughie" who soon recovered and found her way to the mission.

Monção, a border town in the north of Portugal, was the yellow bus's first stop, where the team met their first Brazilian missionaries. It's been nearly forty years since then and hundreds of tent missions later, and Pops is finding it impossible to remember each individual mission – but he will always remember those Brazilians!

It was as if the Brazilians had been in the house of Mary, Martha and Lazarus when they made Jesus supper, as John describes in his gospel. Mary's and Martha's brother Lazarus, whom Jesus raised from the dead, was sitting with Jesus while Martha served the supper. Mary poured her very costly perfume over the feet of Jesus and the fragrance filled the whole house and gradually fell on the disciples. When the disciples finally left the house, they must have carried something of that fragrance with them into the world.

It seemed to Pops that those missionaries had been in the same kind of place where Jesus was loved and worshipped, and they were still unconsciously carrying that incredible experience.

Parades de Coura, a small town not far from Monção, was chosen as the site for the first tent mission. The tent went up without any problem except one! "Pull" in English is "Puxa" (pronounced "Pusha") in Portuguese. Pops, as everybody knows, is fluent in most languages and had gotten the hang of Portuguese in the first couple of days in the country.

"The secret," he told Nana, "is just put an "o" on the end of every other word and everyone will understand."

"Yes, dear," said Nana.

So Pops thought he had to correct the lovely young Portuguese English student who was relaying his instructions to the people helping with the tent.

"Pull," said Pops.

"Pusha," said Paula, the student.

"No, no! Pull!" said Pops louder.

"No, no! Pusha!" said Paula.

Pops shouted even louder, Paula started crying and Nana came to the rescue, persuading Pops that he might not have the grip on the language that he thought he had.

"Obrigada," said Paula.

"De nada," said Nana.

"Oh," said Pops.

The first meeting, and every other meeting, was crazily fantastic: they would never finish until midnight or later, with lots of singing, shouting and dancing inside and outside the big tent. All the Brazilians and their children were at every meeting.

Joed and Naome, with their three small children, lived at the edge of a forest in a breezeblock shack with no electricity.

Ananias and Lilia and their four children seemed to feed the whole town and the team with a few fish and a couple of loaves of bread (sounds familiar?).

Jailson and his wife Lucia, who was pregnant with their second child, together with their two-year-old boy, lived in a very small mobile home. They sold it when a family that was saved during the mission said they could dig out a cave underneath their house and live there, so that they could look after the church that had just been born from the mission.

There was a single lady, Maria Pirez da Luz, who had planted churches in Portugal and Angola: Pops heard not long ago that when she retired back in Brazil, she decided she didn't like retiring, so she travelled to the north of Brazil and planted some more churches!

And finally, but not least, there was Helcio, a young man who didn't arrive until later in the year. He spent his first night sleeping on a platform bench, and later became the best interpreter Pops ever had. And because he could do the "Ossie Ardiles" trick, jumping over a football then flicking it up back over his head, he immediately became Peter's hero.

Although those missionaries had given up houses, lands, friends and jobs, they were full of joy, fun and a red-hot love for Jesus - and, to Pops's surprise, they all had some idea of how to play football, which made his work much easier!

Over the next few years Pops, Nana and the family took many teams to Portugal. Sometimes many were saved, sometimes just a few, but always there was that atmosphere of love and faith, and Pops knew that those people had been with Jesus.

Joed and Naomi are now back in Brazil looking after a large city church.

Ananias and Lilia have recently just escaped with their lives from the Amazon, where they were chased by illegal loggers with machetes and spears.

Jailson and Lucia moved to Poland where they planted a thriving church in Bialystok and invited Pops to hold tent missions there.

Helcio married a lovely girl who came over with Pops's next team to Spain and Portugal; they have lived in Portugal ever since, planting churches and raising a gorgeous family. Pops was very proud when Helcio asked him to be his best man at their wedding. Pops's speech brought tears to the eyes of the guests; it was not because it was very moving, but because he still thought he could speak Portuguese just by adding an O!

Gloria a Deus!

22
LITTLE BLUE BAGS

Pops's dad liked his pint and sometimes on a summer evening he would drive Pops's mum, sister Denise and Pops in his trusty Morris Minor (definitely an improvement on the Austin 7) into the countryside to one of his favourite pubs. To be one of his favourite pubs, it only needed one thing - to sell Bass beer. He was a lifelong supporter of team Bass and in return he would always find a warm welcome in any house with the red triangle over the door.

If the evening was fine, then the whole family would sit in the beer garden. If it was raining, Pops's mum and dad would disappear inside the pub, his dad with his pint of Bass, his mum with a Mackeson, and then his dad would bring out a bag of crisps and a bottle of Vimto to Denise and Pops in the car. (Children were not allowed to go inside pubs in those days.)

Now inside the bag of crisps (plain of course) was always a small blue bag of salt. You had to fish it out from among the crisps, being careful not to rip it, then untwist the blue bag and sprinkle the salt over your crisps, so producing your own do-it-yourself ready salted crisps. Pops would eat his crisps as quickly as possible in the hope of persuading his little sister to give him some of hers - a tradition that is still very much alive in the Orange family!

Now the point of the story, if you were wondering, is this: the bags of salt were not introduced first of all to make the crisps tastier (though that would make a good sermon), but to make the person eating them thirsty. If you are thirsty, you are going to drink more beer and if you drink more beer, that is going to make Mr Bass very happy - clever Mr Bass!

These little stories are Pops's blue bags - he wants to make you thirsty, more thirsty, not for beer or Vimto, but for Jesus.

Pops was saved when he was eighteen; now he is seventy and he is thirstier for Jesus than he has been for a long time. Writing these stories has made him thirsty to know Jesus like he's never known Him before. There is a verse in the book of Job that talks about "the edges of His ways" and that's what these stories are. It's like the sick lady who just managed to reach out and touch the hem of Jesus' coat and was healed. Pops was stretching out as far as he could, and the more he stretched he knew that God was bigger, greater and more wonderful than he could ever imagine.

At one time in Leamington, Nana and Pops rented a very nice house from some lovely friends. Every evening after tea Pops would be upstairs in the bedroom praying; sometimes Nana's friends would visit her and Nana, as she always did, would make tea and cakes - but then all of a sudden they would hear very loud shouting coming from the bedroom and her friends would jump and even sometimes spill their tea.

"What's that noise?" they would ask Nana.

"Oh, it's only Dave praying," Nana would answer.

"You don't pray like that!" they would say, a little alarmed and a little worried for Nana. But Nana would just say, "Dave does" as if it was the most normal thing in the world.

Pops had read about a man in the Bible called Jacob. God had really blessed him; he had two beautiful wives, lots of sons and lots of servants, thousands of sheep and cows - but still he wasn't satisfied, for he knew there was something more.

One night, when he was alone, an angel in the form of a Man came and wrestled with him and as it was getting light the Man said, "Let me go for the day is breaking."

But Jacob said, "I will not let you go unless you bless me".

The angel said, "What is your name?"

"Jacob," he replied.

The angel said, "It will no longer be Jacob but Israel, because you have struggled with God and with man and have prevailed" - and in that struggling, God had changed Jacob.

Pops felt a bit like Jacob; he knew God had really blessed him, although he hadn't got any servants, sheep or cows and only had one wife (which was more than enough!).

But somehow, he knew there was more. There was God, just God and not Pops. As far as Pops could understand, God was saying to him, "It's either Me or you" - and that's what all the shouting and praying was about. It was just a little man with a big thirst praying to a big God, who could satisfy that thirst by flooding that little man with Himself, and little Pops would be swept away in the flood.

Nana's Prayer Cake Recipe

- 50 parts Faith
- 48 parts Desire
- 2 parts Tears
- Plus, a dash of shouting, only if required!

23
TWO WITNESSES

The word 'Geek' wasn't invented when Pops was at school but if it had been, then John would have been one. He enjoyed Maths, English and History, he always did his homework and was always getting A's and B's for everything except, of course, for games. Pops had never ever talked with John.

Pops somehow had been persuaded to go to see a rock band from Liverpool called The Crossbeats.

"From Liverpool," Pops thought, "Cool!" (Another word that hadn't yet been invented but Pops was light years ahead of his time!)

The word 'Cross' should have given Pops a clue to the trap he was walking into, but it was too late: the band had started playing, and anyway there were lots of girls there so it wasn't going to be that bad, he was just going to keep his head down.

Then it happened - someone was calling him chicken, although not quite in so many words. One of the guitarists was saying,

"If there is anyone brave enough to find out the claims of Jesus Christ then they should come out to the front and talk to one of the group."

Pops just couldn't resist the challenge; he couldn't have cared less about the claims of Jesus Christ, but he wasn't a chicken, so out he went. But - a big mistake! John, the geek, was there talking to people about Jesus - he was a Christian! Pops looked for the exit and before the trap was sprung, Pops escaped.

John, it turned out, wasn't just a Sunday Christian, he was a Monday Christian too. In Monday lunch break Pops was in the playground with his mates, playing a game that is apparently illegal now. His mates were all bigger than he was but because Pops played rugby with them (scrum half) and because he could be cheekier to the teachers than the rest of them, he was well in.

John walked right up to Pops, pushing through his mates, and said, "Do you still want to talk about Jesus?"

Pops was stunned and did the only thing he could do, swore at John a lot! He made a stupid joke to his mates and turned his back on John, hoping he would never see him again and that his mates would never ask what that was all about.

Late at night, when Pops did most of his thinking, he had to admit to himself that John the Geek had a lot more guts than he had ever had, and he felt ashamed, but luckily there was another day, another stupid joke and another game to play. It took another three years before Pops stopped the stupid jokes and came to Jesus, but John had planted the seed.

*****

Suceava is a town east of the Carpathian Mountains in Romania. It was the last night of a week's tent mission; all the local churches had been involved and many people had opened their hearts to the gospel. Amongst the people who had responded, Pops spotted an old lady dressed all in black, shuffling forward, waiting for someone to talk to her. When Pops looked again over the heads of the crowd, he could not see her and presumed she had gone home.

Pops liked to go back to the places where missions had been held, to see how people were doing and if they were going on with Jesus. Pops asked about the old lady who had responded on the last evening and this is what he was told.

She had travelled back to her village and immediately started telling everyone what had happened to her, that Jesus had come into her heart and made her happier than she had ever been. But a lot of the villagers, especially the local Orthodox priest, didn't like what she was saying and threatened her to keep her quiet. When she didn't stop talking about it, they threw bricks at her little cottage and broke all the windows.

In response she hired a minibus and took as many young people who wanted to go into Suceava to the youth meetings that had started after the mission.

To thank her for being so kind to the young people the priest persuaded some of the local bullies to drag her out of her cottage, tie her up and hang her upside down by her ankles from her own apple tree and then beat her with rods.

She was so grateful she started a youth church in her cottage. When all the young people from the village and surrounding farms flocked to her cottage, the priest and the bullies had to stop their persecution because of fear of being chased out of the village by irate parents who had seen such a change in their children.

Pops still doesn't know the name of that little old lady, but Jesus does.

24
A YELLOW DOOR TO GO WITH THE YELLOW BUS

Nana said that Pops mustn't knock down any more walls in their house or the whole house would fall down.

"But Pen, trust me, I'm a builder," said Pops.

"No more," said Nana.

"No, dear," said Pops. The problem was that even with his 'Open Plan' and with people sitting on the stairs, no more than a hundred people could squash into the Jesus meetings.

Nana and Pops had had to leave the 'very nice' house that they had rented and started to look for a house to buy for themselves and the church to meet in. They had found 4 Wise Terrace, the cheapest house that would accommodate a pregnant Nana, one-year old Daniel, Pops and a girl who had been thrown out of her home.

Having been turned down by all the building societies, they went to the council to ask for a 100% mortgage.

"Sorry," they said. "It's under a demolition order so there's no mortgage available."

"Well, we will just go to a higher authority," Pops told the man behind the desk.

"Sometimes, Dave, I think it would be good not to say everything that comes into your head," Nana said to Pops as they walked home.

A week later (and this is still a mystery to Nana and Pops) although he was allergic to supermarkets, in fact, allergic to any shop that didn't sell tools or fishing rods, he found himself walking through Sainsbury's. Well, in there he bumped into the owners of Wise Terrace who said they were sorry he didn't want the house.

"We do want the house but it's due for demolition," said Pops.

"No, it's not," they replied, "and we will sort it out." And sort it out they did!

Nana and Pops got their mortgage, but still not enough to buy the house; they had asked for £6000 and been given £5000.

But the owners said, "That's OK, we will lower the price to the mortgage they will give you."

Over a year later, Pops discovered that other people were also trying for the house but were also told it was under a demolition order. Soon after they had moved in, BT purchased the other half of the building to demolish it and make an underground tunnel for a new telephone exchange.

By the time all the work was finished, including giving Nana and Pops three new rooms, the microchip had been invented and the new exchange wasn't needed, so BT let Nana and Pops use the remaining land for a garden.

But now, some time after all that, Pops wanted a bigger place for the church to meet. He had read a book by Oswald J Smith called 'The Passion for Souls'; as soon as he saw the title, he knew he had to read it. In one chapter, Mr Smith said, "Why do so many churches hide away in back streets when there is a whole world to win?" Wise Terrace was certainly in a back street and although lots of people had found No 4 and been blessed, there were hundreds who hadn't!

"The church must have a door on the high street so the whole town can be reached for Jesus," said Pops.

"Good idea," said Nana and "Praise the Lord!" said Pops.

The church started praying. Brochures from estate agents started piling up on Pops's desk but there was nothing suitable. Brochures, papers, pamphlets – Pops was getting frustrated. Nana, who was now an expert in recognising the signs of a coming volcanic eruption, took over and found a night club for lease.

They went to see it: all the walls were black, with huge hell's angels, ghost riders, skeletons, skulls and crossbones painted on the walls and carpets that felt like peat bogs. But the best thing of all was that the front door opened directly on to the High Street at the main crossroads of the town - perfect!

But there was one problem: the police had raided the nightclub and called the fire service in, who promptly closed the whole place down because of fire risks. It was going to cost thousands of pounds to build a fire escape over the neighbouring properties (for the rooms were upstairs) before the fire chief would even consider opening it again.

The church prayed and on Monday morning Pops visited the

fire station to get an interview with the Fire Chief.

"Yes, he has a free five minutes, so go on in," said his secretary with a smile or a smirk, Pops couldn't tell which.

"What do you want, son?" asked the Chief. Pops looked at him and then at his desk and noticed some architect's plans for the closed night club rolled out on the desk.

"I want that night club."

"Well, you can't have it, I've closed it down, fire regulations."

Pops thought of something to say but decided against it, he had learnt his lesson; all he could do was stand in front of the Chief and wait.

"What do you want it for?"

"A church," replied Pops.

"Oh well, in that case you can have it – there are no fire regulations for a place of worship."

So Pops had got his door onto the High St.

It took the church six months, working every night and some working every day as well, to get South Town Christian Church ready for opening. The last thing to do was to paint the door a very bright yellow. And Pops just couldn't help mentioning to Nana that it always helps to go to a higher authority!

25
THE GOOD, THE BAD AND THE MIRACLE

Pops felt that he was in the middle of a 'Spaghetti Western Movie.'

He was in Mexico and Xavier, his friend and interpreter, had been driving for a couple of hours. By the time Pops got up to preach (standing on four orange boxes) it was pitch black and all he could see of the congregation, apart from a few horses hitched up to posts, were the first two or three rows - mostly Mexican men, some wearing cowboy hats, others with droopy moustaches, one or two wearing old Bruce Willis vests, but all of them, much to Pops's relief, were not holding six-shooters but were carrying Bibles!

The meeting, as far as Pops could tell, was being held in a very big garden or orchard of some kind. Pops was preaching about the resurrection and how the angel told the woman, "It's no good looking for the living amongst the dead because Jesus is alive!"

Then a thought popped into Pops's head and he said, "You know God has commanded His disciples, not angels, to preach the gospel to the world." Suddenly it seemed that the whole congregation were on their feet cheering and clapping and hugging one another. Pops hadn't got a clue what was happening. After a while the people calmed down and the meeting eventually finished with some kneeling and praying with tears, others singing and dancing. Pops decided he liked Mexicans.

As people started to make their way home, the leaders asked Xavier if they could tell their story to Pops.

"It will explain about the angel," they said.

The five leaders of the church invited Xavier and Pops to what Pops presumed was going to be a restaurant, but it was a "Spaghetti Western" salon, complete with swinging half doors, a long bar and men playing poker. Pops was hoping to see someone chewing tobacco and saying, 'Do you feel lucky, punk?' but he realised he was getting his films mixed up.

Over very hot tacos and gallons of coke the leaders told their story.

"We were all black magicians but we wanted more power; we were told to go to a certain mountain and meet with other witches and the chief witch would appear and give us more power. So we set off for the mountain, but halfway there an angel appeared to us and said what we were doing was against God's command and dangerous, and we should go back home and read a Bible."

None of the men had Bibles so they asked the local Roman Catholic priest for one, but he refused. After travelling to the nearest big town, they were able to buy five Bibles and they started at Genesis and read all the way through the Old Testament.

Then they prayed, asking God to send His angel again to explain what they were reading. The angel came and told them to carry on reading into the New Testament, which they did.

The got through Mathew, Mark, Luke and John and onwards into the Acts of the Apostles - and then when they started reading Acts of the Apostles chapter two, God baptised them in the Holy Spirit and they became new men!

Soon their wives, children, uncles, nephews, nieces and neighbours were being saved and joining what they now realised was a brand-new church, the one Pops had just preached in.

The angel appeared once more to them and amongst the things they were told was that it was the job of the church to preach the gospel to the world, and there would be 'a gringo' coming across the water to tell them more about Jesus and Pops was that man. That's why they got so excited about his comment concerning the angel and the empty tomb.

If anyone had told that story to Pops, he would have found it very hard to believe, but he stayed with those men for three weeks, was with the church every day and saw how they lived, their great love for God and for one another, their desire for holiness and for the lost. Pops knew he was witnessing something very special and truly amazing.

After the men had finished their story they asked, "What happened to you at 4 o'clock yesterday? The Spirit spoke to us all separately to meet together and pray for you because you were in danger."

"At 4 o'clock yesterday," Xavier told them, "we were driving down a mountain in the car I brought from the States when the engine stopped, all the brakes failed, and the power assisted steering failed! Miraculously the car kept on the road until we reached the valley bottom!"

Although Pops didn't know it, this wasn't going to be the last time that invisible hands kept Pops and his friends safe from dodgy bridges, frozen rivers, mud slides, runaway trailers and many more near-disasters. But Pops reckons the safest place to be is in the will of God, and Nana thanks God that her husband whom she loves very much (despite him thinking he looks better in a vest than Bruce Willis) is being looked after by a mighty God.

26
FIVE CROWNS

Story no.1

"You need Jesus." Nana was sharing a flask of coffee with her friend whom she had got to know at the typing class.

Nana was the only one who could decipher Pops's hand writing (still is) but typing out his letters with two fingers was just taking too long. Pops tried suggesting that she could type them when everyone was in bed, or when the house work was done, or when she'd finished all the paper work for the church, or had sorted out the latest homeless person sent by social services (first with a bath then a meal and then a bed, always in that order!).

"I'm taking typing lessons," said Nana.

"Yes, dear," said Pops.

So Nana, after hearing about all her friend's trials and difficulties, knew the only answer for her friend was Jesus. Nana invited her to the "Praise and Testimony" celebrations at the church's new night club on Saturday evening. There, while she was listening to the gospel of Jesus, she said a great big YES to Jesus and her life totally and wonderfully changed. And God has powerfully used her ever since.

Story no.2

The marquee was full and buzzing with activity: in one corner there was a children's Bible class, and in another corner people were being helped in their first few days of becoming Christians, in another part of the tent there was an impromptu gospel meeting of local people who were curious about all the things that were happening. Pops happened to look up at the tent entrance and noticed a lady on her own, nervously looking around.

Pops went over to her and just said, "You want Jesus, don't you?"

"Yes, yes, I do," she said and there and then she gave her life to Jesus and Jesus gave His life to her.

Story no.3

The young Polish lad was coming to the kids' meetings in the afternoons. The Big Tent was on the site in Poland where fifty years previously the whole Jewish community (the second biggest in the country) had been rounded up by the Nazis, loaded onto trucks and taken to the railhead and from there to the concentration camps.

The young lad didn't know anything about that but he did know that Jesus loved him and died for him, and halfway through the mission he gave his young heart to God; although he had a goitre as big as a football round his neck, joy was just bursting out of him!

"Can Jesus take this away?" he asked Pops. "My father put this amber necklace around my neck to cure it, but nothing's happened." The goitre had started growing not long after the disaster at Chernobyl, which was only a long day's journey from where the tent was.

"Yes, He can," said Pops. "But first, go home, tell your dad about Jesus and ask him if he will take the necklace off. Then come back and we will ask Jesus to take that thing away." And off he ran.

Pops was afraid he had asked too much of the lad and wondered if he would see him again, but there he was in the evening meeting with no necklace. Pops and his friends prayed, and the lad went home quite happy that his friend Jesus had heard.

The next morning while the team were having breakfast, the lad appeared "Look, it's completely gone!" - and so it had, you would never have thought that there had ever been anything there. This is our Jesus.

Story no.4

A young gypsy man who was preparing to marry his beautiful fiancée came up to Pops after a tent meeting and said, "I want what you have, mister."

"Well, what I have got is Jesus," replied Pops.

"Then I must have Him."

With tears in their eyes they prayed through together and

the young man received his reward - eternal life.

Story no.5

Matthew was there again at his usual place, sitting behind his desk collecting taxes. Nothing would shift him from his task of extracting the last mite that was due from the fishermen, merchants and all who traded along the shores of Galilee - even though it meant listening to the words of the teacher who was preaching from one of those fishermen's boats. He was surprised that he could hear the words as clearly as he could but thought it must just be the wind blowing off the lake, carrying the words to his ears, and, although he didn't realise it, sowing them in his heart.

Suddenly the preaching stopped - or was it that the wind had changed direction?

Matthew looked up and was fixed by a pair of eyes that were on fire.

The preacher said, "Follow Me" and Matthew left his table and his money and followed, and for two thousand years millions of people have been blessed by Matthew's account of the Son of God.

Jesus said, "The harvest is plentiful, but the labourers are few. Therefore, pray the Lord of the harvest to send out labourers into His harvest."

(Matthew chapter 9 v 37-38)

27
THINGS THAT COME TO LIGHT

There are lots of things that have happened on missions that Pops knew nothing about.

For instance, some time ago Pops was persuaded against his better judgement to get a dog.

"We will all take it for walks, dad."

"Yes, for a week," Pops said, "And then what?"

"Oh, let them have a dog," said Nana, so the Oranges got a dog.

Someone suggested calling it 'Chewbacca' out of Star Wars.

"That would be a great name for a dog," said Pops.

"No, no, that's not a good idea at all!" cried the kids in unison and then they all looked at each other with the kind of grin that said, 'We know something that you don't.'

What they knew was that one of the names the young people called Pops on mission was indeed 'Chewbacca.'

"Chewbacca? Why Chewbacca?" asked Pops.

"Because that's what they said you sounded like when you

were shouting instructions when the tent was going up or coming down or unloading or about to leave or crossing a border or...."

"OK, thank you, kids."

Pops tried to look shocked, but he was thinking 'Chewbacca eh! Cool' - he hadn't a clue who Chewbacca was! Dozens of names were suggested, so Nana decided to call the dog Sam.

A more edifying story Pops heard of not long ago had happened in one of the missions in Moldova.

Because there were so many people responding to the gospel and coming forward to be spoken to and prayed for, Pops was worried someone might fall over and get trodden on, so he asked those who weren't coming forward to leave the tent. Everywhere he looked, people were praying, some with tears of repentance, some clapping with the joy of sins forgiven.

While all this was happening, Lis, one of the team, was praying for a lady, when suddenly the woman interrupted her, saying to the interpreter, "This young girl speaks very good Russian. Where did she learn?"

Lis couldn't actually speak a word of Russian; she was praying in tongues but in perfect Russian, and God was blessing the lady speaking to her in her native tongue. Now Lis has a great husband and a wonderful son, and Pops is quite sure she wouldn't dream of calling Pops 'Chewbacca'!

The team had returned to one of the towns in Kalmykia where the previous year they had held a mission. As usual in that part of Russia, any foreign trucks had to report to the local police station and an armed guard would be placed around the truck until morning.

As the team were starting breakfast there was a knock on the door and a mother and daughter appeared, whom the team recognised from the previous year. It was wonderful to see them again and obvious that they were excited to see everyone. No sooner had they sat down to chat, when others appeared at the door, this time a film crew from the regional TV. They had heard the team had arrived back and wanted an interview with Pops, but before he could say anything, the mother said, "I'll speak to them." So, the cameras were switched on and off she went:

"One year ago, Jesus came to our town and many of us were saved, and now we all have a beautiful church and a good pastor. Last year the doctors told me I had very bad cancer and nothing could be done to help me. We went to the big tent and heard about Jesus healing people and watched these people laying hands on some of our friends and praying. I couldn't go to the front, so I told my daughter just to do what that man was doing so she put her hands on my head.

"I went back to the hospital and this time they couldn't find anything wrong with me, no cancer, no nothing! Buddha hasn't done anything for us [a lot of the townspeople were Buddhists] but Jesus has washed us clean and healed us. And many other people have been healed in the town because we told our friends and neighbours what Jesus could do, and they were also healed when we prayed for them."

When she had finished Pops asked how they knew the team were back in town.

"My daughter woke up the other morning and told me she

dreamed the Jesus people would be arriving tomorrow, so here we are to welcome you."

The 'good pastor' of the church had arrived nine months after the mission. He had been on a YWAM (Youth With A Mission) course back in the Ukraine. At the end of the course, the teacher asked all the class to pray individually, asking God where He wanted to send them. The young man couldn't get a clear answer except for a strange sounding word popping into his head. So, he went to the teacher to ask what he should do; he advised him to have a look in an atlas and see if he could find it. Wonderfully it was the very town where the mission had been and where the beautiful new church was now!

28
A HORSEBOX FOR THE GOSPEL

It had to be big enough to sleep five children and two adults, strong enough to carry five tons of marquee and equipment and still have enough space for at least one month's food for a team of twenty. Horses are big and heavy and need something pretty strong to transport them and their owners, so obviously a horsebox was what was needed.

Second-hand Bedford TL 7.5tons: **£5,000.00**

New Horsebox sleeping 7 with provision for all the mission equipment: **£10,000.00**

Total: £15,000.00

Answer:

Sell house in Leamington

Buy cheaper house in Liverpool

Remaining money **£15,000.00**

Job Done.

Although maybe none of the church in Leamington got to travel in the new horsebox, Pops and Nana knew that without their prayers and sacrifice the move from Leamington to Liverpool would never have happened. Pops believes it was in South Town Church that the Holy Spirit separated him and Nana to the work He had called them to; many of these little stories happened because of the faithful and sacrificial lives of their friends.

One of the first missions the Bedford took part in was taking aid to some of the churches in Romania that had been persecuted under the dictator Ceausescu. Pops and his two very good friends, Micky and Terry, visited about seven churches around Romania, distributing food, clothes, Bibles and money.

One church had been praying for money so they could put windows in their building. They had been meeting for years, summer and winter, without any windows and with very little heating; winter temperatures can go down to minus 25 degrees Celsius. When Terry gave all the dollars that had been given from the churches in Liverpool, there were lots of tears, hugs and kisses - and Romanians really know how to hug and kiss! It was an experience that was new to Pops and his friends; all three would get two kisses on both cheeks and one full on the lips by all the pastors of the churches.

It was also decided that Pops's eldest son would marry the pastor's eldest daughter; Pops would supply the tent for the outdoor ceremony and the pastor would supply the goat for the wedding feast - but the two young people had other plans and it never happened!

Shame! Pops was looking forward to eating roast goat in his marquee, but he had to admit the kissing may have gotten a little out of hand.

Every morning the 'three amigos' would discuss who would be the driver that day but when it was time to fire up the Bedford, it seemed that Pops usually forgot what had been decided, plonked himself in the driving seat and off they would go. Micky and Terry miraculously are still some of Pops's closest and very gracious friends. A lady called Jo wrote a song about how a young man wouldn't let his best friends play with his new toy: it's called 'Driving Dave's Lorry,' and it's a classic.

The Romanian orphanages were soon discovered, where thousands of 'Ceausescu babies' had been taken from their parents who had been 'encouraged' to have as many children as possible to build up the nation's population and armed forces. When the parents couldn't feed their children any more (because most of the food grown in Romania was transported to Moscow), the babies were taken away from them and placed in orphanages all over the country. Some of the conditions the children were living in reminded Pops of his time working in the zoo, but the smell of stale milk, soiled clothes and filthy beds was far worse. Those children old enough to stand would just rock back and forth in their cots all day.

On one such trip taking aid, Pops was with men from Liverpool. They would call themselves hard men, and seemed unmoved when every morning he would give a short talk on the love of God - but when they witnessed these children most of them broke down in uncontrollable sobbing; Pops learnt later that some of them had become Christians.

Driving home again on the autobahns through Germany, Pops was in his own little world. He couldn't drive and talk at the same time as he got confused, but he could pray. He asked the Lord, "Should I keep concentrating on taking aid?"

The Lord answered very clearly, "Your main mission is to take the gospel. The gospel is the only thing that can change a nation, so preach the gospel."

So that's what Pops did.

29
A BIG LESSON FROM A LITTLE MAN

"What's going on, what's happening? I knew I wasn't an evangelist; I knew I shouldn't have given up driving a tractor! We've come all this way, and no one saved! I'm useless."

Pops was in a sorry state: he knew that Christians ought not to have black moods so maybe he wasn't a Christian after all, maybe he was just fooling himself.

Pops and his daughter Ruth were holding a mission in a small railway town in the east of Poland and as usual kids were pouring into Ruth's 'Kidz Klub' every afternoon. Right from the beginning God had blessed the children's work and Pops still hears of people whom God had blessed in Ruth's Kidz Klubs, now going on to be leaders in different churches all over Europe and beyond. It was no surprise to Pops that the children's work was so successful - it was because Ruth lived close to Jesus and Jesus was able to shine through her and the kids loved her. She even loved Pops when he was in his grumpy moods - incredible!

It was the last night of the mission and, unlike the kids' meeting, the tent was barely half full. Pops had been struggling to pray all day, right up to the time of the evening meeting. When it was time to get on his feet to preach his heart felt dead and his mind a big block of wood with a few woodworm in it for good measure.

Pops cried out in his heart, 'Lord help me' and immediately the words came to him: 'Talk about your friend.'

Now Pops knew what to preach about: his friend Zacchaeus. He was a very little man who wanted to see Jesus, but because of the crowds he was finding it impossible, so he ran on ahead and climbed into a tree. When Jesus and the crowds reached the tree, Jesus stopped and looked up and said, "Zacchaeus, come down, today I must stay at your house."

And right then Pops saw something he had never seen before: Jesus was in the centre of a huge crowd but when he got to Zacchaeus' tree Jesus, the Son of the Almighty God, stopped and looked up to this little man that all the town hated (he had made himself rich with some very dodgy tax collecting).

It was the same when Jesus was washing Peter's and the disciples' feet at the last supper: He must have looked up at each of them, even though he knew they would desert Him and even deny they knew Him.

And again with the woman who had been dragged into the temple and accused of adultery when Jesus was teaching there. Jesus stooped down to write something on the floor: He must have looked up to her too.

At that moment, Pops knew God wanted him to look up to all men, not just treat them as a crowd who needed the gospel, but as they were, individuals with their own secrets and fears, whom Jesus had died for because He loved them with all that He was.

That night, in his heart while he was still preaching, Pops was saying sorry to the Lord that he was forgetting the reason why he was called to preach the gospel.

That night one person responded to the One who stopped and looked up, and she invited Him into her heart.

Sometime later Ruth lived in Poland for a year establishing a 'Kids Klub' and that very same girl who courageously responded on her own became Ruth's chief helper. When Ruth finally left, this girl took on the responsibility of the work with a wonderful missionary couple from Brazil.

And Pops had learned a little more about Jesus's mighty love.

30
OH LORD, WON'T YOU BUY ME A MERCEDES BENZ?

Oh Lord, won't you buy me a Mercedes Benz?

(Sorry, kids, an old Blues classic)

Nana's hands were covered with black greasy oil, her perfume was a sweet delicate essence of diesel oil and half her body was hidden in the engine cowling of the Bedford. Pops had lost count of how many times the Bedford had conked out on the way back to England from their last mission trip. Now it was only fifty miles until they reached the ferry port at Calais and it had happened yet again!

Diesel fuel wasn't getting through to the engine and it needed bleeding again, so Pops was buried on one side of the engine, slacking off the injector pipes, and Nana was on the other side, pumping the manual diesel pump until all the air had been pushed out of the fuel, then tightening up the pipes, hoping the engine would fire up and get them to the terminal in time for the last ferry.

Oh, and there was a gale blowing, that Mr Fish (the BBC weatherman) said was not going to happen, but it was already uprooting trees, pushing walls over and driving rain into every part of the Bedford's engine!

When Pops finally climbed back into the driving seat and was turning the key, hoping to hear that beautiful noise of a diesel engine firing up, he looked over to Nana's red eyes and her tears mixing with black grease running down her face - and then he knew (no, not to settle down with his wife and children, this isn't a romance novel) - it was time for a bigger and better truck!

Pops had been told he was overloading the Bedford: he now had bigger generators, seats to sit three hundred people, more lighting, bigger sound equipment and of course a bigger marquee - and the old Bedford was struggling. The truck that had caught Pops's eye while driving on the continent was the Mercedes draw-bar, a sixteen-foot truck towing a sixteen-foot trailer with a capacity of thirty-eight tons: a monster compared to the 7½ ton Bedford.

The first thing Pops had to do was pass his Class 1 driving test and then start praying. In October he found exactly what he was looking for in Leeds - a one-year-old Mercedes with hardly any miles on the clock. The dealer had just sold one, exactly the same, to the Blue Peter Appeal for the Orphans in Romania. The cost: £21,000 plus a new suitable trailer and plus payment for somebody to take the body off the Bedford and fit it onto the new chassis.

Pops had read about the life of George Muller, a man who had looked after thousands of orphaned boys and girls, not only building beautiful houses for them but clothing, feeding and educating them. Muller believed the only person a Christian had to ask to supply the need of God's work was God Himself. So Pops decided that if what he was doing was what God wanted him to do, then God would supply all that was necessary for his new truck.

Pops told the dealer he hadn't got any money but God was going to supply all he needed by the end of January, so would he keep the Mercedes until then? The dealer agreed - the first miracle, a Yorkshire man agreeing on such a deal!

The only people that knew about the Mercedes were the incredible sacrificial small full-time team that worked with Pops, and the prayer meeting at Devonshire Rd Church in Liverpool which the Oranges belonged to.

The weeks passed and slowly money from different people came in, but it was nothing compared to what was needed. One Saturday morning Pops was standing in the living-room, leaning on the Welsh dresser, looking out of the window, waiting for Nana to shout that lunch was ready, when the Holy Spirit said, "If you want that truck, you need to get it before lunch."

Pops knew what he had to do: he went upstairs to his little study, got on his face before the Lord and prayed. By the time Nana shouted, "Lunch," Pops KNEW the Mercedes was his!

Pops always looked forward to Friday mornings, when he went to speak to the Upper School at the Christian Fellowship School. The school had always been a tremendous inspiration and blessing to Pops, not only to God's faithfulness but also to the sacrificial service of Christians with a vision to give children a Christ-centred education.

Most of the kids there had Christian parents and had preaching and preachers coming out of their ears, and some were a little bit cynical about these things. What could Pops say to them that hadn't been said already in a much more eloquent way?

This time Pops decided to take a photograph in to show them the truck that was being prayed for.

"By the end of January," he said, "I will own this truck. It costs £21,000 and at the moment I have got £125!"

"That's a lot of jumble sales, sir."

"Are you going to have raffles, sir?"

"No, we are just going to pray. The only people who will know are the team and the prayer meeting and now you, so don't go telling anybody, and when we have it you will have to admit that God answers prayer," Pops answered.

There was a lot of smirking and a general consensus that this bloke was a bit weird.

Every Friday Pops would appear with his photo and bring an up-to-date account of the Truck Money.

"That's still not very much, sir. Are you sure you know what you're doing?"

Pops thanked God he did know what he was doing, or else he would not be standing in front of a bunch of sarcastic fifteen-year-olds. God bless them!

The end of January arrived and with it, God's wonderful provision – praise God! – but minus £5. Nana and Pops were pretty sure that the Leeds dealer wouldn't quibble over £5. They were about to get into the car for the journey over to Leeds when Trish, a friend from the church, came running down the street with an envelope in her hand.

"I know it isn't much," she said, "But while I was praying this morning, I am sure the Lord asked me to give you this."

Nana opened the envelope and there was the £5! Any drivers passing by might have observed three very happy Christians having a little dance in the street. Jesus - His name is faithful and true.

Back in the classroom nothing much needed to be said, God had proved His point to those young people. Pops hoped that those same young people would dare to prove God in a thousand more ways than Pops could ever dream of doing.

31
OCEAN OF LOVE

Pops wasn't sure if the sweet old lady was crying because she was sad or because she was happy. The meeting had finished and Pops and the team were talking to some of the people who had responded to the gospel – Muslims, Buddhists, Russian Orthodox, Communists and, of course, atheists, all wanting to know more about this Jesus who had died for them and risen from the dead.

As soon as Pops saw an interpreter who was free, he grabbed him and pulled him over to where the old lady was sitting. (Sometimes at the end of a meeting getting an interpreter was a bit like playing British Bulldog: if you weren't quick enough someone else would catch them and then you would have to wait in line until they were finished - Pops wasn't very good at waiting in line but better at grabbing them!)

So, the old lady told her story of when she was sixteen years old and her younger brother fourteen. One night in Kalmykia at the end of 1941 the Red Army soldiers had knocked on her family's front door and demanded to be let in. You certainly didn't argue with the Red Army soldiers.

"You have twenty minutes to pack a suitcase, then come with us," was the order from the soldiers.

Then they were marched to the railway, put on rail wagons

which headed out east to Siberia. Every day their wagon door would be opened, and soldiers would check if any of the 'passengers' were sick. The sick ones would be thrown out and left at the side of the rails. By this time the train was over the Urals and into Siberia, the temperature was well below freezing and many were falling ill, including our friend's young brother. She did her best to keep him warm and hide him from the soldiers, but one morning he was discovered, ripped from her arms and thrown into the snow - that was the last she saw of her young brother.

Although she had done everything she could to protect him, for the rest of her life she carried the guilt of seeing her young brother lying in the snow, knowing that in a few hours he would have frozen to death.

The old lady finished her story and then said, "But tonight God's love has come into my heart and washed my guilt away - at last I am free!"

Pops tried to explain that it wasn't her fault that she couldn't save her brother, but he could see that God was doing something wonderful in the old lady's heart and so he just kept quiet and watched God love His child.

Later Pops asked his Russian friends to explain the background of her story.

After Hitler invaded Russia, Stalin was afraid that the Kalmyks would side with the Nazis, so he decided to get rid of all the Kalmyks, as simple as that. You can always trust Communism to come up with a nice simple solution to any problem.

"Death solves all problems - no man, no problem."

- Joseph Stalin 1918

"I saw also there was an ocean of darkness and death, but an infinite ocean of light and love which flowed over the ocean of darkness. And in that also I saw the infinite love of God."

- George Fox 1647

32
SOMEWHERE IN SIBERIA

For the third time that morning Pops had stopped the truck.

"There's still something wrong, Graham. Can you have another look at the brakes?"

Eight sets of wheels means a lot of brakes but Graham, undaunted, jumped down and started crawling under the truck and trailer, checking all the wheels and brakes. It had been a sunny morning which meant the road (really just a track) that ran from the eastern side of the Ural Mountains to Kazakhstan, was drying out, so that when Graham emerged from under the truck he wasn't quite as muddy and wet as he had been the first time!

"Everything seems fine, Dave - can't see anything wrong," and there it was again, that great big Jesus grin.

Pops knew that if it wasn't for Graham and the rest of the team, there wouldn't be any 'All for Jesus Missions.'

"OK, let's go!" shouted Pops as he fired up the truck. Because it was a decent bit of road that morning, the truck was able to whizz along at all of 25 miles an hour. Sometimes the road was so bad that the team could walk alongside the truck to stretch their legs!

But after ten minutes, Pops knew something still wasn't right.

"If it's not the brakes, check the trailer coupling," Pops shouted, as yet again he brought the truck to a halt.

"I'll go," said Marcus. "Graham's still changing his clothes."

Pops decided to get Marcus to walk between the truck and trailer to see if there was any movement in the coupling. Suddenly Marcus appeared in Pop's driving mirror, frantically waving his arms and shouting, "Stop, stop! Come and see this!"

By the way, it's not recommended that anybody should walk between a 16-ton truck and a 16-ton trailer, especially on a dirt track in the middle of Siberia. What Pops saw made his stomach churn (and he had a pretty strong stomach). The big 7x4 inch steel that the trailer coupling was bolted to had completely broken its weld on one side of the chassis and was swaying back and forth with the movement of the trailer. If Marcus hadn't spotted it then, at any moment the trailer could have ripped away from the truck and caused a horrific accident.

The trailer had to be unhitched immediately so that the truck could go in search of someone who could repair it well enough to travel the 4,000+ miles back to the UK.

There was one small problem, though - which way to go?

The team hadn't seen anyone or anything in two days. Because the Russian authorities had made sure there were no reliable maps to buy 'for security reasons,' the only map Pops and the team had was the souvenir map Marcus had bought years ago on a school trip in St Petersburg. It showed the whole of the USSR on a piece of paper no bigger than a handkerchief

- good old Marcus! They just knew that if they kept heading west, eventually they would hit Moscow.

Pops decided to keep heading west, hoping that sooner or later they would come across a town or village with someone capable of doing the repairs. It was decided that Chris and Clive would stay in the Land Rover and guard the trailer. Pops made sure they had enough food and drink to last them at least three days.

"We don't know how long we will be, so go easy on the food and of course you can sleep in the trailer."

"Oh, don't worry about us, we'll be fine," said Clive. Pops looked at Clive and knew they would.

"Yes, boss, we'll be fine," Chris repeated, with half an eye on all that lovely food.

And so Pops, with the rest of the team, jumped in the truck and set off to find a welder. The team were unusually quiet, probably praying. Pops thought that the Lord would look after Clive and Chris. Bev, Clive's wife, was probably praying that Chris wouldn't eat Clive!

Suddenly the Spirit spoke to Pops: "There's a track on your right, turn down it now."

Immediately there was the track and Pops swung the truck into it. After two or three hundred yards a huge quarry opened up in front of them. Pops pulled up in front of a wooden hut that looked like some kind of office, with five men sitting on a bench leaning against the wall of the hut.

Pops jumped down from the truck and one of the men said in perfect English, "Can I help you?"

"Yes, please, we need our truck repairing," replied Pops.

"Can I help you" was the only English this man spoke, and Pops knew it was time for Jo and her 'talking book' to take over. (Over the years Jo had compiled notebooks full of words she had picked up from hundreds of conversations in dozens of countries.)

So, with the help of Graham holding an imaginary welding rod and doing 'Zurrr' noises, and Jo using her amazing ability to communicate, the men saw the problem and said that Yes, they could fix it.

With the help of sign language and Jo's 'speaking book' the people in the office explained that some of the big equipment was down and all the men, including the welders, were not able to do their work, so they were very happy to help the English people.

"A lucky coincidence," they said. Jo said she believed it was God who had arranged that the welders would be free to help the English with their problem.

It took no longer than a couple of hours before the welding was completed and, as far as Jo and the team could understand, all of the welders plus everyone in the office had received the Lord with much joy and tears. After exchanging gifts, a couple of Nana's fruit cakes for the quarry people and a bottle of vodka for the team (kept in the team's stores as a first-class substitute for anti-freeze!), Pops turned round and headed back to Clive, Chris and the trailer.

What Pops was expecting to take at least two days had taken less than four hours. Jesus said, "Go make disciples of all nations - and I am with you always." He had proved Himself, yet again, totally faithful.

After arriving back in Liverpool Pops told this story to a friend of his, Alan, who had done a lot of work on the truck and trailer. Alan told him that because the Russian welders were used to very heavy machinery, they were the perfect men to repair the truck, and the job they did could not have been better done.

Clive told Pops some months later that as soon as the truck disappeared Chris became very hungry, and by the time the truck returned all the two days' supply of food had been eaten! Pops said he was just glad Chris didn't eat Clive.

Chris is still going for Jesus, working in the townships in South Africa, a disciple with a heart as big as a football and a huge appetite for the glory of God.

33
OUT OF THE MUD

Incidents of a Wally

1. Most people Pops's age can tell you where they were the day President Kennedy was assassinated. Pops was in an ambulance being rushed to hospital after careering into the back of a parked car. In the hospital the police asked him how it had happened, but Pops said he couldn't remember - concussion. It had happened when the kids from all the three schools on Myton Rd were let out at the same time at 4 o'clock. The police asked for witnesses in the assemblies of all three schools. Some girls (not from his school) said that he was on his bike, looking behind him, gesturing and shouting things at them and didn't see the parked car. Some people said Pops was 'accident prone' but Pops knows he was just a 'wally.'

2. A car door opened, and Pops, not looking where he was going, rode straight into it and somersaulted over the top - the judges gave him 9.5!

3. Pops knew the front light on his bike wasn't working properly but hadn't got the sense to do anything about it; a car overtaking him at night crashed into him, his handlebars went into his liver and spleen and he broke his arm. The surgeon told his parents to prepare for the worst: he survived but was off work

for eighteen months.

4. Pops drove the work minivan too fast in the snow, crashed and destroyed a telegraph pole.

5. Pops did a 'ton' (100mph) in his boss's wife's MG, showing off to a couple of his mates; he was spotted by his boss's friends, and as it was the last in a list of stupid things, Pops got the sack.

6. Pops drove his tractor too fast round a bend and the silage trailer full of tons of grass tipped over.

7. Pops drove the farmer's tipper truck too fast and ended up in the back of the contractor's combine harvester.

8. Pops turned right without looking when driving the big Plough Master tractor and a passing car bounced off the big tractor wheels.

9. The article in the local paper said: "Mr Orange said it was safer to drive on the pavement than on the road." Noticing a policeman on the other side of the road, he gave him a friendly wave. Pops was in a hurry and parked on the pavement so he could jump out, run into the shop, buy an LP (Bridge over Troubled Water) for his gorgeous new girlfriend - Nana.

10. Pops drove his Morris Minor (with go-faster Pirelli tyres) too fast round a bend and collided with a car whose occupants included three policemen!

11. And finally, Pops took Nana on a date, for a nice drive in his Morris (with go-faster Pirelli tyres) when a sports car overtook them. Pops took up the challenge, accelerated, thinking that if he took a short cut, he should be able to get in front of the bloke

who had dared to overtake Pops's Morris (with go-faster Pirelli tyres). But Nana had had enough - she leaned over and removed the ignition key, the Morris shuddering to a halt.

"Are you really a Christian, Dave, because sometimes you don't act like one?"

Pops was embarrassed. "Sorry, Pen, it won't happen again," and it didn't.

"He who finds a wife finds a good thing and obtains favour from the Lord."

Proverbs 18 v 22

Now Pops was leading a team driving a 40ft, 30-ton truck across Siberia. God's delight is to make Wallies into new creations and so sure is He of His work, that He gives them the honour and privilege to serve Him. Pops loves God very much.

The truck had been stuck in the mud for two days - even with the snow chains on they weren't budging an inch. A quarter of a mile down the track there were half a dozen other trucks in the same predicament. The team decided to pay them a visit, so with a few Russian Bibles and Nana's famous fruit cake, they set off, slipping and sliding, to make their introductions.

The Bibles and fruit cake were gratefully received in exchange, of course, for Russia's finest anti-freeze, commonly known as vodka!

"What do you do when the mud is like this and you can't drive?" asked Pops.

The Russians pointed up to heaven and said, "We wait until God brings the sun out but listen…"

They became very serious: "You must not go around the next village; it's very dangerous after it's been raining, just carry on straight through the village."

The next morning there was a blue sky, the sun was shining, and the team got ready to go. Pops asked the lads to take the Land Rover into the village to see if the truck and trailer would be able to get through. Sometimes the houses were so close together and the track so bad that it was impossible for the truck to go through the centre of a village.

The lads were back within half an hour with the news that the ruts were at least 2ft deep and it would be impossible for the truck to get through. At that time the truck had only two-wheel drive; later it was fitted with four-wheel drive and with much higher ground clearance. There was only one way to go, and that was around the village.

The Land Rover set off first and found the road skirting the village. Clive called up on the CB radio, "Dave, the track suddenly falls down to a bridge over a river, steep banks on either side of the track, so be careful."

Pops told the rest of the team to get as far back in the truck as they could, to put as much weight as possible on the back wheels. The truck started heading down towards the river; if Pops braked, because of the mud would lose control of the truck, so he just had to keep going.

Pops looked in his mirror, hoping to see just the far corner of the trailer as usual but the trailer was actually taking up most of his mirror. It was jack-knifing, and in a few more yards it was going to slip off the track, down the embankment and pull the truck with it into the river - which, of course, because of the rain was a rushing brown torrent!

Pops shouted back over his shoulder to the team, "Pray, pray now!"

Then he heard a booming voice, it had to be Marcus.

"Lord, send your angel now!"

Immediately they all heard a loud bump on the side of the trailer. Pops looked in his mirror and saw the trailer straighten up and follow the truck as it ought to do in a straight line - and then they were safely on the bridge!

Pops looked down into the torrent below and knew without a shadow of doubt that again God had kept them, and he worshipped the God who said, "Go and I will be with you always."

The only problem now was how to drive up the other side. Pops called up Clive on the CB radio and he seemed to know what Pops was thinking.

"No problem, bro." (That was one of Clive's favourite sayings.)

Pops looked up and saw a huge tractor waiting to pull the truck up the bank, which, he realised, was a lot gentler than the one they had just come down.

"He also pulled me up out of a horrible pit,

Out of the miry clay,

And set my feet upon a rock,

And established my steps."

Psalm 40 v 2

34
WAKE UP

It was Sunday morning and, as usual, Madge was getting ready to go to her church, where she would be worshipping the God who had saved her, and praying for her husband who needed saving. Eddie, her husband, would also be getting ready to go out, but he would be going down to his allotment to spend time with his beloved pigeons.

Madge's passion was Jesus: Eddie's passion was pigeon racing. Madge's church was well known in Otley; it was a bit like Marmite - you either loved it or hated it; it was definitely not lukewarm! You either loved it because the vicar and his church worshipped Jesus, or you hated it because the vicar and his church worshipped Jesus - and just to make sure you couldn't sit on the fence, the vicar hung a banner at the front of the church, saying "This Church is for Sinners Only."

One night, Eddie had a dream. He was between two angels who were dragging him down a long straight road. At the far end of the road he could just make out the form of a cross. Somehow, he knew that was his destination. He struggled to get free, but the angels' grip was too strong.

In desperation he cried out to the angels, asking, "Why are you doing this?"

One of them replied, "Because of these," and pointed to either side of the road.

When Eddie looked up, as far as he could see on both sides of the road there were billboards, each one depicting a scene of Eddie's life. Some of the scenes showed things that Eddie had done; others, things that he had said; and still others, things that he had thought and wished for, that had come from deep in the darkness of his heart - and all the time he was being dragged nearer and nearer to the cross, realising they were going to nail him to it. At the same time, he knew somehow that he more than deserved the punishment that was soon to take place.

As the angels were preparing to carry out the sentence, a man stepped forward and said to them, "Let him go. I have taken his place."

Then Eddie woke up.

Eddie and the vicar became very good friends, and later on, with their families they both moved down to Leamington. The vicar was the one who told Pops he was banned from the church until he was changed, and he was the first to welcome him back when he did. Eddie more than anyone else was the one who helped and guided Pops in his first years of Christianity. At Nana's and Pops's wedding the vicar married them and Eddie preached.

The apostle Paul writing to his friends in Rome said, "God commends His own love towards us in that while we were still sinners Christ died for us."

35
SPECIAL DELIVERY

The Siberian family lived in a small village surrounded by birch trees and mud. For a long, long time they had been praying for a Bible so they could learn more about the God of earth and heaven; they didn't know anyone who had one, and to travel to the nearest town was impossible, so they kept on praying and waiting, believing that somehow God would answer their prayers.

Then one night the youngest daughter had a dream. She dreamt that some English Christians knocked on their door with Bibles in their hands. So, believing that was a dream from God, they decided to make a big sign over their double gates, saying, 'Jesus Loves You', and then they waited some more.

Every three days on their journey over to Mongolia, Pops would send the Land Rover into a nearby village to buy bread and to look for a well where the truck could fill up with drinking and washing water. If it looked as if the truck would be able to drive up to the well, the Land Rover would either call on the CB radio or come back and tell Pops the situation.

This particular village was about a quarter of a mile down a small muddy track that led off the main muddy track.

"Ok, off you go, kids, and, by the way, see if you can get hold of some asbestos rope so that we can stop the exhaust from blowing."

Pops liked to hear the Mercedes V8 engine quietly singing along; he wasn't too fond of the exhaust making a racket.

The general concession was that Pops was just a little bit mad – never in a million years would they be able to get hold of a piece of asbestos rope for his beloved truck in the middle of Siberia. On reflection, however, Pops wonders who was the maddest: Pops who wanted to drive the length of Russia just to say hello to the missionaries who had presented themselves to God as a living sacrifice, or those who had decided to go with him!

The Land Rover group found the well but couldn't find anywhere that might sell bread. And then right in front of them there it was in big red letters: 'Jesus Loves You.' Hardly believing what they were looking at, the team got out of the Land Rover, pushed the big gates open, walked through the farmyard and knocked on the front door.

The door was opened by a young girl who looked at them, shouted, started crying and ran back into the house, soon to reappear with the rest of her family. Now all were shouting, crying, dancing and hugging the team who were then dragged inside and made to sit down. Lots of food and drink appeared on the family table (no vodka) and everyone started talking at once.

Gradually, Jo with her "speaking book" started to understand what had happened. The same faces that the young girl had seen in her dream were the faces that had appeared at her door and now were enjoying the very best of Siberian hospitality.

Jo said to Mark, "You'd better go and tell Dave what's happened and don't forget the Bibles." (There was always a good stash of Bibles in different languages kept in the truck.)

Half an hour later Pops and the rest of the team were joining in the celebrations and enjoying some excellent home cooking.

After Pops felt that the team had done sufficient justice to the tasty food, he asked them, "Have you asked about the rope? We need to get going." (In those days Pops was always in a hurry.)

No, they hadn't and were hoping Pops had forgotten all about it.

"How do you translate, 'Please have you got a piece of asbestos rope that you can give us for the exhaust of the truck' from English into Russian when I don't speak Russian and these lovely people don't speak English?" Jo said to Pops, giving him one of her looks that she had perfected over thirty years of teaching young children.

"If anybody can, it's you, Jo," replied Pops, with more than a little sympathy for Jo's past students.

Five minutes later and Jo had again done the impossible: the father got up from his chair and beckoned Pops to follow him. They went out of the house and into a barn close by. When the father opened the doors, Pops could see the barn was empty except for a few cans and one or two hand tools.

The father led Pops to the only window in the barn and pointed to something on the window sill. When Pops looked, he saw a foot-long piece of asbestos rope, which the father picked up and gave to him. Pops knew it had been lying there a long time because it had left a perfect mark in the dust.

Out of all the things that the father and his family could have prayed for, they had asked God for His book. They didn't care about any western toys that they thought the English could have brought. To them the written word of God was more precious than gold, and when his daughter was given the dream, it was just God saying, "Don't worry, it's on its way."

An hour later, and Pops again was listening to the sweet singing of the V8 engine without the accompaniment of the exhaust, pulling Pops and the team eastwards, worshipping the God who always delivers on time.

36
IT'S NOT WHAT YOU KNOW, IT'S WHO YOU KNOW

Pops and the team had been parked up on the Siberian side of the Mongolian border now for three days. The Russian Army captain in charge of the border had told them they might as well turn round and head back to England because there was no chance they would be allowed though his border: NO British truck had ever driven through his border and Pops would not be the first.

Pops told him, "We've driven seven thousand miles to get into Mongolia and we're not going to turn back now, you will see!"

Every time the guards changed duty they would make a point of having a good laugh as they marched past the truck, convinced of the invincible Red Army and its power over all its people and borders; but Pops and the team were praying, still convinced of the Name that is above every name, the name of the One who was dead and now is alive for evermore and has the keys to any border that He wants to open.

It took Pops most of the day to get through to Nana on the phone in the local Post Office (a long time before mobiles were even thought of) to ask her to call the church to pray and to see if she could contact the British Embassy in Moscow.

The next day Pops rang again and heard Nana's story: after

spending many hours on the telephone and talking to dozens of officials, she finally got through to the British Consul in Moscow, who said that that very evening he was due to attend a banquet and would speak to his friend who was the head of all the Russian border staff, which he did. Not only was he the chief of the border staff, but in his younger days he had been the captain of the exact border where Pops and the team were stuck.

"Just tell them at their convenience to drive up to the border and I guarantee they will get through."

Now here was something you don't see every day: the truck slowly came up to the border barriers, and all the guards on either side of the road were standing to attention and saluting. The captain opened the cab door and very politely invited Pops and the team inside the guard room to drink tea while the paperwork was checked and passports stamped. After another glass of tea and some very sweet biscuits, the captain came in to say everything was in order and he hoped Pops and the team would have a very happy time in Mongolia! Then, with more shaking of hands and saluting, the barriers were lifted and the truck drove the fifty yards to the Mongolian side of the border.

The truck had only moved fifty yards but it could have been a thousand miles: everyone was smiling, bowing and politely directing the truck into a parking bay. A Mongolian guard smiled, made a sign to switch off the engine and then nothing - everyone disappeared. The team decided it would be best to do the same and politely and quietly wait for someone to come and attend to the paperwork but after an hour there was no sign of anyone. Pops could see there was a slow but steady stream of cars, all of them second-hand Toyota 4x4s, moving through the border and he realised that they were being ignored.

Pops then collected all the team's passports and the truck's paperwork and set off, armed with wise advice from the rest of the team:

"Dave, be patient, be humble, be polite, be careful, dad, be cool, man"- that last from Clive, Dave's co-driver and sanctified ex-hippy.

Pops had learned over time some of the secrets of getting through borders and dealing with officials and uniforms:

1. Give the impression you know what you're doing

2. Give the impression you know somebody high up in authority

3. Never take no for an answer.

Well, only rarely did Pops know what he was doing but he did know the One who said, "Go and I will be with you," which had given him the confidence to look for a 'Yes' and not a 'No'.

Pops got himself into the chief's office and after another hour of smiling and lots of 'No's' there was a breakthrough.

"OK, OK, interpreter, interpreter he come." Picking up his phone the chief, Pops hoped, called for an interpreter to travel up to the border.

After another hour or so a young man in uniform knocked on the door of the truck and came in. After a nice friendly conversation and inspecting the inside of the truck, Pops asked the interpreter,

"What must we do to be allowed into your country?"

The interpreter replied, "You have very big writing on your truck saying 'All For Jesus Missions' but we are a Buddhist country, so it is not wise."

"What shall we do then?" Pops asked again. The young Mongolian army interpreter looked at Pops and said, "I have read your book three times; you must pray."

When Pops looked at that young man he realised he was looking at a brother and both the young man and Pops with tears in their eyes hugged each other and then the rest of the team joined in! (The book, of course, was the Bible.) He then took all the paperwork and passports to be stamped.

Pops and the team took the advice of their young brother and prayed; within an hour all the paperwork was completed, passports were stamped, and barriers were lifted, and the truck was driving in Mongolia, heading towards Ulaanbaatar.

That was twenty-five years ago, and Pops has never seen his young friend since, but one day they will meet each other again in the Kingdom where every citizen has just one stamp in their passport:

'This one has been born into the Kingdom of God and Jesus Christ is their Lord and Saviour.'

37
LAYLA THE BRAVE

The team were spending the night in Rostov-on-Don, the town of the last Pentecostal Church in the Ukraine before crossing the border into Russia. After making sure everyone had been fed Ukrainian style and had everything that was needed for a good night's sleep, the best of all being a good hot shower, Vladimir told Pops,

"There will be two interpreters coming tomorrow morning before we leave: please interview them both and pick the one you want. God bless you; we'll see you in the morning."

Vladimir was a hero of the persecuted church in Ukraine and the one who would lead Pops and the team into Kalmykia, a small autonomous country on the shores of the Caspian Sea.

As Pops walked back to the truck, he felt the Lord say, 'The interpreters will both be ladies, one with dark hair and one with blonde hair; pick the one with blonde hair.'

When Pops told that to the team they suggested that he should have a good night's sleep and hopefully he would feel better in the morning! He had to admit it was a strange thing for the Lord to say.

"It's probably all the driving making me a bit light-headed,"

Pops said, trying to assure the team he wasn't going even more crazy.

While the team were having breakfast the next morning, Vladimir introduced the two interpreters to Pops. They were both ladies, one with dark hair and the other blonde. Without interviewing either of them Pops chose the blonde-haired lady.

"Are you sure, brother Dave?" Vladimir asked. Pops was sure.

The team christened her Layla because her Russian name was so long that none of the English could pronounce it. Because of the Kalmyks' very conservative culture, Layla was sent home to change into something more suitable for a seven-week mission and to offload all her earrings, necklaces, rings, bracelets and make-up.

Vladimir and his team had been planning this mission for over a year and had made several trips into Kalmykia, arranging with local authorities and securing permission to erect the marquee in the different locations. This had demanded a lot of sacrifice and involved not a little danger when they had to battle with suspicious soldiers, blizzards and snowdrifts during the long Russian winter.

Right from the start it was obvious that Layla was an excellent interpreter, despite the fact that she had never seen a Bible before and hadn't got a clue who Jesus Christ was. But with the help of Vladimir she learned very quickly, and by the second mission she had understood that eternal life was available to anyone who would turn from their sin and receive the Lord Jesus who loved them and died for them. Each night she was seeing lives being transformed by the power and forgiveness of God and it was starting to affect her.

The team were half-way through erecting the marquee on the third mission when the mayor of the town rolled up in his car, demanding that the work stop; he had changed his mind. Vladimir soon found out that the local Buddhist monk had told the mayor the Christian meetings must not go ahead. Although the mayor was in charge, he was afraid to go against the monk. Vladimir and Pops decided to travel back to the capital and speak to the authorities who ran the country, and Layla went along to interpret.

The White House, Kalmykia's parliament, was a beautiful imposing building with big marble pillars and marble floors that echoed with the footsteps of anyone daring to enter and challenge its authority.

After explaining their errand, the three musketeers were told to sit and wait. After an hour they were still sitting and waiting. Now this was not good for Pops's blood pressure, but unlike his two friends he hadn't been brought up in a system where if you didn't sit and wait patiently, you would be having an all-expenses-paid holiday in a Siberian gulag with the compliments of the state - and the last thing you would be doing there was sitting!

So, asking Vladimir to pray, Pops took Layla's hand and set off to find some doors he could knock on. After the fourth or fifth a door opened and a Russian voice behind a desk asked what they wanted. Layla, still trembling, told him their story.

The voice behind the desk was charming and asked them to follow him into a lift which eventually stopped on the top floor.

"You can let go of my hand now, Layla," Pops said, giving his hand a quick massage to get some life back into it.

Big double doors were opened and Layla and Pops stepped onto a carpet that really needed snow shoes to walk over, it was so thick. The man behind an even bigger desk stood up and introduced himself as the Minister of the Interior.

"I'm sorry but the Prime Minister is away visiting. I'm sure he would have liked to meet you, and I hope I can help."

Pops never thought knocking on a few doors would have got him this high! "This is God's handiwork," he whispered to Layla and then explained the problem through her.

Again Pops was shaken by the minister's answer: "There is in our culture an old tradition that we would be led to a promised land flowing with milk and honey and when we arrive the God of the heavens would bless us."

Pops, doing his best to control his excitement, told him that Jesus was God's promise to him and his people. He would bless those who put their trust in Him by washing away their sin and giving them a life abundantly full of all the blessings of God.

Pops and the minister spoke to each other for an hour.

Eventually the minister said, "I want you to go all over my country and tell people about this news," and he gave Pops an official paper with his signature and stamp, authorising the marquee to be erected in any place as seemed fit.

God mightily blessed all those six missions, and in the last one brave Layla, who had never heard about Jesus and never seen a Bible, with tears gave her life to Him and Jesus gave His life to her.

Vladimir and his team continued to visit the new churches regularly and witnessed with much joy as God increased His blessings on them all.

38
DISCIPLES

There was a gap of a month in the mission's itinerary and Pops was praying, asking the Lord how He wanted them to use that time. On Friday morning he had been praying and reading his Bible as usual when a scripture in the Acts of the Apostles 'jumped out at him'. In a vision Paul saw a man asking him to come over and help them; the man was from Macedonia. (Acts Chapter 16 v9)

After breakfast, because it was Friday, Pops drove to the Christian Fellowship School to speak in their assembly. As usual he popped into the office to talk to Daphne, the school secretary, a beautiful Christian lady, but someone that even Pops was careful not to mess with!

"Ah, Dave, I'm glad I caught you."

Immediately Pops was fourteen years old again and in the headmaster's study preparing for the worst.

"I've had a letter from friends in Bulgaria," she continued, "asking if I know anyone who could go over to help them with an evangelistic campaign this summer. I immediately thought of you."

"Is Bulgaria kind of where the old Macedonia used to be?"

Pops asked.

"Yes, it is Dave, well done." Pops had got his answer and a merit star from Daphne.

Daphne had met her friends Ivan and Stella two years previously, when she was smuggling Bibles into Bulgaria before perestroika, and when communism had still got a grip on the country. Every morning and evening she had trained herself by walking to work and back with a rucksack full of books and two suitcases, one in either hand, also full of books. If she looked suspicious struggling with heavy suitcases full of Bibles through Bulgarian customs, she would certainly be detained and the Bibles confiscated. But who was going to stop a sweet lady, well over sixty, excited to discover some of their lovely country? She had also had to learn Cyrillic Script and memorise all the addresses of her contacts, because in case of arrest she must not have any written information on her that would endanger her contacts.

Pops can now only remember one or two things about the actual mission, like driving through what was then Yugoslavia and being surprised how clean and well-kept everything was; even the tractors seemed to be polished regularly. Tito was still in charge and compared with the rest of Eastern Europe, it was a pleasant surprise.

There was utter chaos at the Bulgarian border, where hundreds of trucks, cars and trailers were all competing to get through a single gate. Terry, a friend of Pops who had come along with his family, was heroically trying to manoevre his car and caravan so he could remain close to the back of the trailer and Pops, who had all the documents and, most important, all the food.

Driving through the suburbs of Sofia and looking at the endless regiments of shabby high-rise flats, Pops felt sorry for the thousands of people who were living there. When he mentioned it to Stella and Ivan, they explained how, when they had first driven through the same streets, they'd been incredibly happy because they had now at last got a home of their own.

The Lord spoke one morning to Pops saying that in the evening the Lord was going to open the eyes of the blind. Pops mentioned that to the team during the prayer meeting and then, of course, forgot all about it.

At the end of the evening meeting when people were milling about, some being helped and others being prayed for, suddenly there was a shout from a corner of the marquee and two sisters carrying a picture book came up to Pops.

"Look! My sister can see, she was blind but now she can clearly see all the pictures in my book, she can see, she can see!"

When the mission had finished there was a good number of new Christians but no one to look after them. Pops mentioned that to the team. Mark, a young Irish man with the mission for the first time, whom Pops had only known for a few weeks, immediately said,

"If you think I can do it, I will stay behind and do my best to pastor them."

Pops was deeply impressed by this young man who was willing to give up everything he had back in the UK and live in a foreign country amongst people he as yet didn't know - another true disciple of Jesus.

39
SERVANTS OF JESUS

Pastor Ivan had been a coal miner in Ukraine most of his working life; in fact, when the miners in the UK were on strike, as head of his local union he sent a donation over to the UK miners. Some years later he and his colleagues were working barefoot because their boots had worn out and there was no money for new ones; the UK miners' union was asked for help but they never received any reply.

Pastor Ivan was a typical big Ukrainian, 6'2" with broad shoulders and, of course, hands like shovels, but with a very gentle smile and a lovely sweet spirit.

When the call came for miners to help repair the damaged nuclear reactor at Chernobyl, he was one of the first to volunteer. They had to dig under the ground below the reactor that had blown up so that engineers could try to fix the damage without getting fried by the radiation. Many of the miners died and others, of course, developed cancers. Pastor Ivan didn't have to volunteer because by then he was a full-time pastor; he went simply because he loved God and his fellow Ukrainians, and he wanted to serve them.

John with his wife Marion looked after a church in the Midlands and every summer they would travel down to Devon to a Christian conference. The venue was a farm with most of the visitors camping, which meant using a lot of portable toilets. Without going into the finer details, the toilets got very mucky.

John and Marion immediately smelled the need and bought themselves buckets, mops, rubber gloves and nice smelly things and set to work. Every morning and evening you would find them in the toilets. The toilets were kept spotlessly clean now, and Pops always felt bad if he had to walk into one with his muddy wellies on. Very few people knew who it was that kept the toilets clean. Pops knew because he also had to get up early and he caught them with their mops and buckets. Every year they spent their summer holidays cleaning toilets just because they loved their brothers and sisters.

Najua had come to England from Brazil to learn English and then used English to learn Albanian, because that was where she believed God had called her to work. Albania had boasted that it was a completely atheist country and to prove their success the government would hang Christian leaders in the National Football Stadium and play football with the heads of church pastors.

While studying English, Najua lived for a time in Leamington and popped in regularly to see Nana who always was busy with housework, mission work, looking after the church and taking care of the children - and there was always a huge pile of clothes waiting to be ironed, a lot of it being Pops's shirts.

"Why are there always so many of Dave's shirts to be ironed?" Najua asked.

"One minute he is knocking down some wall, the next he is going preaching or visiting someone," replied Nana, doing her best to defend his too frequent changes of clothing.

After that, without asking, Najua became the ironing lady for the Orange family's never-ending washing.

Although Nana's dad spent time at their house and met many of their friends, Nana could never persuade him to come to any of the church's meetings, and he would never raise the subject of Christianity, but the one person he asked about years later was Najua, the lady who did the ironing.

Najua finally got herself into Albania and became one of the first missionaries to raise up churches in the country; she even had her own regular Christian radio programme. When she died a few months ago from the Covid 19 virus, the whole church in Albania mourned for her. She was a legend, but Grandad remembers her because she served Nana by doing her ironing.

Mike was conscripted into the East German Army aged eighteen. He was deployed as a border guard but by that time he had become a Christian and refused to shoot anyone attempting to escape into West Germany. Because of that, for the rest of his National Service he was sentenced to 'Permanent Punishment' until his service was finished.

Pops got to know him and his lovely wife when he was a pastor near the city of Gera. Pops had decided to leave the truck and trailer in Germany between missions, but he needed someone to look after it, garage it, and get it through its MOT. Mike was the one who volunteered. It was only years afterwards, when Pops brought the truck back to the UK, that he realised how exactly much work Mike had done, not only taking care of the truck, but organising new places to garage it and dealing with the mountain of paperwork that went with it, plus feeding mission teams that would descend on his house before sending them off to Eastern Europe.

His wife and his church opened up their hearts to Pops and his friends, always welcoming them, always saying yes to Pops's continual "Mike, could you do me one last favour?" Pops used to kid himself it was because of his loveable personality that Mike kept agreeing - but it wasn't. It was Mike's great heart.

"If anyone serves Me, let him follow Me; and where I am, there My servant will be also. If anyone serves Me, him My Father will honour." John Chap.12 v.26

40
WELLIES, SLIPPERS, PEN AND OTHER THINGS

Twelve years ago, a young friend of Pops said to him, "I believe God is saying to you 'Put your slippers on and rest'"

"Rubbish," said Pops, "I want to die with my boots on, the devil can keep his slippers."

Rob, Pops's brave young friend, stood his ground: "Well that's what I believe the Lord has said, Dave."

Over the next few months, the Chronic Fatigue got worse and worse until finally Pops found it difficult to get out of bed, and the only thing he could do was rest with his slippers on. Nana not only became his nurse and carer, but also the guard who didn't allow anyone to see or speak to him, because Pops just didn't have the energy to say anything to anybody.

These were dark days, not only for Pops and Nana, but for the children also. Nobody knew what was happening. In Pops's heart, enemies that he had never had to face before seemed to be taking ground from him: depression, unbelief, and an army of a thousand "why's?" surrounding him, but worst of all, the conscious presence of God had left him.

But God never left him, He just disappeared from view. Slowly over the years, through the faithfulness of a faithful God (who although sometimes invisible is always underneath with His everlasting arms), and possessing the most gracious loving wife ever, Pops started to recover.

As Pops was getting better, from time-to-time he would ask God when he could put his boots on again. "Soon but not yet" was the only answer.

In the new year, Nana and Pops visited City Church in Liverpool. Pops's friend the pastor spoke about some of the things God may be calling us to do in the new year (and what a year! it turned out to be the year of the Covid 19 virus). He illustrated his sermon by showing the congregation different pairs of footwear and then he held up a pair of wellies and said, "Someone needs to put on these wellies and get back to work."

Pops whispered to Nana, "That's me; they are my wellies." Pops knew God was going to do something.

Two months later, Covid 19 lockdown started, and because the children couldn't get together in church, Pops wanted to share something for the grandkids, but what? He was doing something in the garden when suddenly the Baby Elephant incident came to mind. The thought was so strong, he had to rush into the house, grab a pen, shout Nana for some paper and start writing. After he'd finished, he looked down and realised he was still wearing his wellies.

From then on, every Thursday and Friday, and sometimes on Saturday, Pops is writing, and Nana is typing. This is something that Pops would not have thought possible in a million years.

For a long time, friends have suggested Pops write a book, but he knew he could never get his head around the idea. But this way, with just one story a week, although in a 'higgledy piggledy' order and a bit rough and ready, it has become possible. Pops even has some friends - Linda from The Wirral and Andy from Bournemouth - doing their best to sort out the proof-reading and editing.

What a marvellous, wonderful, mighty Jesus we have.

"His name shall be called Wonderful, Counsellor, Mighty God, everlasting Father, Prince of Peace."

Isaiah 9 v 8

41
YOU'VE BEEN FRAMED

Russia Pops discovered is a very big country, you can drive hundreds of miles without seeing another soul and what's more to the point of this story is you can go just as far and not see a garage selling diesel and what is an oasis to a camel diesel is to a truck.

The truck and trailer had three fuel tanks, the two on the truck which held sixty gallons each and one on the trailer that held two hundred gallons. That seems a lot but on a good day the truck would do nine miles to the gallon and so when a garage appeared on the horizon everyone would breathe a sigh of relief.

On this particular afternoon a garage was sighted, and the truck sensing diesel turned off the road and headed for the pumps. The garage 'forecourt' was typical of many in Russia about the size of a football pitch. The kiosk/shed the size of a very small caravan and was about 45 yards away from some very dilapidated looking pumps, Pops tried all of them and none of them worked, so Pops sent Marcus ofto the shed to find out what was happening. After fifteen minutes he came back informing Pops that you have to pay first before the pumps are switched on. "How can we know how much to pay until all the tanks are full? Ask him that Marcus". Off Marcus goes again (Marcus's Russian was excellent, he could say 'Spasiba' perfectly like a native just not like a native Russian. This time twenty minutes later Marcus comes trotting back "Think the man says you just have to guess" says Marcus with that boyish checky smile that still from time-to-time haunts, sorry blesses Pops. "Ok" says Pops "Give him as many Roubles you think we will need, and this time take Josephine with you (Josephine with her speaking books was the team's best interpreter) if anyone was going to save Pop's head exploding it was going to be Josephine. Half an hour later Marcus is back "Ok the pumps are switched on" Marcus informs Pops triumphantly. Pops tries again still nothing happening apart from one dim light flickering on and off on one of the pumps all the rest were 'dead as a dodo'. "Ah Ha at last, that will do "says Pops and takes the pump nozzle off the pump, unscrews the cap on the first tank, places the nozzle into the neck of the tank and then nothing not one drop of diesel.

"Now what?" says Pops getting even more frustrated. Pops calls for Graham "Graham please come and fix this pump". When anything breaks, sets on fire (yes, the old Bedford's electrics have in the past set on fire while Pops was actually driving) gets soaking wet or just won't work Graham is the genius who got it all going again. Graham jumps out of the truck with his little bag of tools and sets to work on the pump. It always amazed Pops that how with such few tools Graham could make anything work from a microphone to a generator, Pops was convinced it was Gods anointing on him just like Bezalel in the Old Testament whom God filled with His Spirit of wisdom, understanding and all manner of workmanship (Gen 35).

Forty minutes later and Graham shouted, "Ok Dave it should go now". So, Pops again puts the nozzle back in the first tank "Nothing, nothing, still no diesel "Pops mumbles half to himself half to anybody who is still brave enough to be anywhere near him. "We need to tell Marcus to tell the man to switch the pump on back in the shed" Graham as gentle as he can tells Pops, decerning that Pops could explode at any second. So the rest of the team shout as loud as they can to Marcus "TELL THE MAN TO SWITCH ON". In the distance Marcus is seen disappearing into the shed, another ten minutes later he reappears waving and shouting "It's on, it's on". Pops try's again, still nothing.

To understand what happened next and to have at least a little sympathy for Pops you have to appreciate the team had been away for nearly three months, driving over roads and tracks that weren't on any maps, negotiating broken bridges, spending hours sometimes days dealing with officials, driving over ten hours a day through eight time zones etc etc but most of all Pops being away from Nana for such a long time was not good for Pops and wasn't good for the rest of the team. Pops now totally frustrated takes the nozzle out of the fuel tank and starts to inspect it, lifts it above his head to have a better look inside "There is still nothing coming out" he shouts, then 'Whoosh!' out pours the diesel, in a matter of seconds Pops is soaked in diesel but doesn't move it's like his brain freezes, still he holds the nozzle above his head still the diesel pours all over him. "Turn it off, turn it off" shouts Pops but every time he shouts, he gets another mouthful of diesel. "Dad please put the nozzle into the tank" shouts Ruth coming to her dad's rescue. Pops obeys his daughter and finally the tanks start filling up. The team have now made a circle round Pops trying with all their powers not to start giggling. "Are you ok Dave "asks Liz but of course that was a fatal mistake because as soon as she opened her mouth torrents of uncontrollable laughter poured out, which only started the rest of the team off. Soon stomachs were being held and tears rolling down cheeks, only Ruth managed to keep a straight face and that she confessed years later to Pops took a supreme effort of will.

Pops making himself a 'Diesel Shower' goes down in AFJM folklore.

42
BY ANY MEANS

In stormed Boris (not his real name) marching round the tables with his big Doc Martin boots on, a bottle of beer in one hand, a West Brom supporters scarf folded in half and twisted very tightly in the other, viciously swirling round his head. If the customers in the Christian coffee bar in Leamington avoided being christened by stale beer, there was still a good chance they would get blessed by the swinging hard ball inside the scarf in the other hand.

Boris wasn't just a West Brom supporter though; he was generous enough to support all the first division teams equally. On one occasion while visiting his house Boris proudly showed Pops his 'trophies', the scarves of every team in the first division hanging up in his wardrobe.

"They must have cost you a bit," remarked Pops.

"No, not a penny, I just nicked them from the kids coming out of the grounds".

It was a usual Saturday afternoon West Brom had lost again and Pops' friend was drunk. Nana was manageress of the coffee bar but being Saturday and her day off, she was upstairs in the flat with Pops.

There was a knock on the door and a frantic voice shouting "Boris is here, please come down quickly".

Nana and Pops looked at each other and smiled. They loved their friend Boris -he was a bit of a hard case but somewhere inside they had seen something very loveable, even though one time Nana was so angry with him she had deposited one of her famous chocolate cakes all over his head!

When Nana and Pops arrived downstairs into the café most of the customers had wisely disappeared; the one or two of his mates who were left were egging him on and suggesting this was exactly what these Christians needed. Boris was still marching around the café, now chanting at the top of his voice,

"I worship Satan, I worship Satan".

"Boris, what do you think you're doing?" asked the ultimate voice of authority – Nana. Boris stopped dead in his tracks.

"I worship Satan, Penny, he's winning. What has God ever done for me?" and off he went marching again, although now a lot quieter. Boris had made grown men cry and most of the church leaders had banned him from their churches and on more than one occasion had called the police to take him away but he knew it wasn't a good idea to mess with Nana.

Boris had got a job for Pops on the local building site and Pops had had many talks with his friend, usually ending up by Boris promising to follow Jesus. But in a few days' time it would only end up in disappointment when Pops heard of another of Boris's escapades. One talk ended by both of them wrestling on the pavement outside the coffee bar, Pops doing his best to knock some sense into his friend. That was in the very early days of Pops'

Christianity, before he had understood the words that Paul wrote: "We wrestle NOT against flesh and blood." (Ephesians Ch. 6)

"So," said Nana, "Over to you, Dave, it's your turn".

Pops had a flash of inspiration - he hoped.

"Come on, Boris, we're going for a ride!"

"Where?" asked Boris.

"You'll see," said Pops. "Are you coming or not?" Boris loved going anywhere with Pops, so they set off.

Nothing much was said in the car; Boris had calmed down and was enjoying the ride. Forty minutes later they were in the carpark of Coventry Cathedral and walking towards the entrance of the huge new building. Pops didn't care too much about cathedrals - he thought they were a waste of money, especially as The One whom he worshipped was born not in a palace or even in a maternity ward but in a stable, but there was something that Pops had seen at this cathedral that had made quite an impression on him.

Boris and Pops were now standing outside the cathedral and Pops was telling Boris to look up and as they looked up, they saw the huge sculpture of the Angel Michael holding a spear in his right hand and standing over the devil who was bound hand and foot, lying at the Archangel's feet, looking up terrified. "See, that's who you worship and want to serve. He's lost, defeated, he's a liar and he's been lying to you".

Pops could see all the fight drain out of his friend and Pops believed something happened to his friend that day.

When Nana and Pops moved into their first house Boris came to live with them for a time - an interesting year!

Then when Nana and Pops moved to Liverpool, they lost touch with Boris, but one day they had a phone call from him, saying he was in Liverpool helping with a Christian Outreach Mission. Could he come and visit them? The next day when they saw him, they could see straight away he was a changed man, a lovely, gentle man, loving God and serving Him and worshiping the one who has the victory - Jesus.

43
THE CROWD FOR CHRIST

Pops had a friend who for a time in the late sixties was part of a harvesting crew in America. In late summer they would begin in the southern states of America with their huge combine harvesters, tractors, trailers and no doubt endless supply of Big Macs and gradually work their way north following the ripening of the wheat until they reached the Canadian border.

It was hard work, starting early in the morning as soon as the sun had burnt the dew off the corn and then all through the day and, with their powerful lights switched on, late into the night. They worked the combines so hard that halfway up America the combines had worn out and they would sell them and buy brand new ones.

Not far behind the combines would come the ploughs, then the cultivators, then the drills (sowers) and then, after a well-earned rest, another harvest would be ready in the south, the combines would be serviced, fired up, turned around and off they would go again.

One wet summer in Poland, while Pops was running a tent mission, he had the privilege of being a 'roadie' for a couple of days to a rock band who were working with the mission, the fabulous 'Supervision'. They had finished one gig in the afternoon and Pops was rushing them to their evening gig (cool, eh?) when something caught his eye; he slammed the brakes on the Land Rover and eventually it shuddered to a stop (it's not a good idea to perform an emergency stop with a Land Rover full of rock band and assorted instruments!)

"Quick, everybody out and have a look at this field," Pops ordered.

Everyone jumped out.

"Look at that, what a waste," Pops said.

"What are we supposed to be looking at?"

" What's happening?"

"What's wrong with your dad?"

The questions were directed at Pop's daughter Ruth and, not for the first time, Ruth hadn't got a clue what her dad was doing.

"Look at this field of wheat: it's ruined with mildew, the wind and rain has battered it flat and it's rotting away. Even if the combine could get into the field hardly any of the wheat could be saved, the harvest is lost, it's too late." Pops was mostly speaking to himself and to anyone who may have been listening.

"Come on, kids, jump back in, there's work to be done," and off the Land Rover raced to the next gig. (By the way 'Supervision' are the best Christian band ever.)

Pops had realised a long time ago that there is a harvest to be won and a much more important harvest than just wheat, a gathering of the peoples of the world to Jesus, that they might know Him and receive eternal life. He knew he must preach the gospel as much as he could to as many people as he could and God had given him tents, trucks, trailers and all the other paraphernalia needed to preach to the fields of people.

Pops knew he wasn't that much of a preacher; he also knew that many of his contemporaries thought he was going over the top in his pursuit of making an 'evangelism machine', but he discovered a book called 'The Crowd for Christ' about the history of Cliff College, the Methodist Evangelical Bible School. Just the title was enough to convince Pops he was on the right track, a track that took him in a different direction from many of the brothers and friends that he loved very much, but as some of Pops' stories testify, God has proved Himself one hundred percent faithful.

Pops can see that there have been some wonderfully God-inspired initiatives and movements in recent years, equipping and inspiring the body of Christ in personal evangelism and they have been very successful; but he believes the gospel must be preached publicly in the vast marketplace of humanity by men and women filled with the Holy Spirit, who can say, like Peter and his friends in the days of Pentecost:

"This is that which was written........" "Jesus Christ crucified........" "Who God has raised up from the dead and exulted to His right hand........" "There is no other name given among men by which we must be saved but the name of Jesus..."

Pops' prayer for his younger brothers and sisters is that, after this horrible pandemic has passed, there would be those who take up the challenge, get hold of the boldness of the Holy Spirit, be filled with the love of God and be a fool for Christ' sake and preach Jesus and him crucified.

44
LABOURERS LABOURING

Monday 10.00hrs - Liverpool

Twenty-six fresh faced young Christians raring to go.

Two of the best youth workers Pops knew: Bernard and Jackie and their two children.

Two dedicated pastors of the church: Pete and Sue and their two children.

Pops and Nana and their five children.

One 56-seater AEC coach just bought second hand and serviced to transport all the above.

One 44ft Mercedes truck and insulated trailer, transporting marquee, seats, generators, food, camping tents, sleeping bags, luggage, etc.

Monday 20.00hrs

Have crossed the Channel and arrived in Hazebrouck, Northern France. Prepared evening meal for 40 hungry travellers and sorted out sleeping arrangements: boys at the front of the trailer, girls at the back of the trailer, curtain in between. The oldies and under 10s in the truck.

Tuesday 7.00hrs

Prayers, breakfast on the road at 10.00hrs heading south.

Wednesday and Thurs ditto

Friday 23.00hrs

Arrive outside church building in Porto, Portugal.

Young people very hot, very tired, very hungry, most of them smelly. It's quickly realised that the team is not really wanted by the leader of the church in Porto, so Pops phones the headquarters of the Brazilian Mission in Portugal. Their immediate response lovingly says, "Please come and all stay with us tonight and we will work out tomorrow what to do."

Saturday 02.00hrs

All bedded down for the night.

Saturday 07.00hrs (no lie-in on mission)

After prayer and breakfast, Ananias the leader of Antioch Brazilian Mission says he has spoken to a young missionary couple who have recently arrived in Portugal and would be thrilled for the team to hold a mission in the town where they have set up home.

Saturday 11.00hrs

Arrive in Felgueiras and meet Getulio and his wife Graciola who already have permission from the owner of a private piece of land opposite where they live for a site for the marquee. It's a good site, maybe half the size of a football field, but it's overgrown with brambles and shrub.

Saturday 16.00hrs

Finished clearing site using any tools that are available, most effective being the marquee's steel stakes. Lots of blisters and scratches, a new experience for some of the young Christians. ("Do 'em good," comments Pops.) Jackie and Sue dispense sticking plasters, etc. Nana makes supper.

Sunday 09.00hrs

After breakfast and prayers, start erecting marquee. Lots of shouting of orders. "Always takes longer with a new team," says Nana to a surprised Sue and Jackie.

Sunday 19.00hrs

After washing (half a bucket of water only, lucky ones scrounging a shower at Getulio's.) Pete with his guitar leads the team singing through the streets of Felgueiras, inviting people to the meeting. Dozens of local people follow the music into the marquee.

Sunday 19.45

Marquee packed with people, standing room only at the back. Many already starting to respond to the gospel.

Sunday 23.00hrs

Tired but rejoicing, bed down for the night.

Monday 9.00hrs

In prayer meeting someone reads the account in Acts of Paul in Corinth. Believe the Lord has many people in the town. Acts 18 v 9-10.

Afterwards young people start to organise visiting and practise dramas, singing and arrange an afternoon children's meeting for every day of the mission.

Monday 19.30

Meeting starts.

Monday 19.45

Town Mayor arrives and asks permission to speak. "Uh, uh," says Pops to Nana. "What have we done wrong this time? Is he going to close down the mission?"

Bernard who is leading the meeting hands the mike over to the mayor.

The mayor says, "When we first saw you English arrive in our town we were afraid you had come just to get drunk and cause trouble. But when we saw you young people work so hard, and how friendly you were towards us, we had to change our minds and now we have heard your message of Jesus we know that is what our town needs. We are very glad you came and you are very welcome. Please continue with as many meetings as possible."

From then on everyone in the team was invited for meals with different families in the town and (a bigger blessing!) they could even use their showers anytime they liked.

At the end of two weeks many had experienced the

forgiveness of sins and the life of Jesus flooding their hearts, and others had been set free from addictions and witchcraft.

Monday 6.00hrs (2 weeks later)

Pops makes everybody get up to make an early start to break camp and take down the marquee. Nana tells Pops it's too early and there is no need to rush, but he takes no notice.

With everything packed away, the vehicles checked, and all the team accounted for, they say their goodbyes to the people in the town and especially to Getulio and Graciola.

Pete and Bernard, their families and the team head back to England. Pops, Nana and children head to the next mission.

Saturday 17.00hrs

Team arrive back in Liverpool. Sometime later, Pops was told it was like watching folk stepping off the coach from a war zone: all of them were exhausted, some of them were still carrying bruises, one even had his arm in a sling, but all of them had incredible stories of seeing how God can move and how He can transform lives and, Pops hopes, some with a vision for the future.

Four months later

Pops travels back to Felgueiras to see how things are doing. He finds hundreds of people packed into one of the town's large meeting rooms, many of them singing and praising the Lord, standing clapping, others on their knees praying. When Pops begins to speak one or two start screaming, so he tells the evil spirits to shut up and leave and things become quiet and they all enjoy the lovely presence of the Lord.

Over an evening meal Getulio tells Pops what used to happen before the mission. Two coachloads of folk from the town used to travel to another town to attend spiritualist meetings, but since the start of the church at least two coaches every Sunday are now travelling in the opposite direction to spend the day with the Christians in Felgueiras.

Getulio and Graciola have their hands full but they are rejoicing in what God is doing.

45
NOTHING FORGOTTEN

A note from a reader.

Thanks Dave and Penny

Very nice to read that account in last week's story. I remember clearing the ground for the tent that time very well. I had been using a bit of thin steel concrete reinforcing bar that I had found on the ground to hack at the weeds, and when I looked at my hands which were blistered and beginning to bleed, I felt really good. I was doing something for the Lord, something that was costing me a bit in a small way, but it was very precious to me at the time, as was the whole mission. It felt like we were back in Bible times and the gospel was doing its work in a very real way - which you were probably well used to, but it was quite new to me in that mission context. It was fantastic. It was there I learnt more to throw myself into the practical work, and I cleaned the loos and even ended up under the bus at one point, fixing the exhaust on with some wire! It was my first mission trip with All For Jesus Missions.

I'm surprised at Dave getting details about the truck wrong though! It was the Bedford you had then, the Mercedes came later as did the larger trailer which boys and girls slept in on different sides of a curtain! On this mission I think the girls were sleeping in the coach and the lads were on the ground outside.

Graham

Because of Graham's eagle eye and his younger memory Nana and Pops thought they had better look through some old photographs of missions and, of course, he was right - it was the old Bedford and trailer and the original canvas tent. The boys slept under the coach or between the coach and truck and the girls slept in the coach, not quite as luxurious as Pops remembers.

Tucked in the photographs there is a picture of a group of young Angolan Christians (this photo must have been taken around 1984-85) who had escaped the civil war that was being fought in Angola, most of them losing both parents in the troubles.

Pops was invited to speak in their Angolan Church which a remarkable lady and her daughter had started just outside Porto. Although Pops felt the Lord had moved amongst them, they were all very cautious and a little nervous. After a few meetings they began to open up and to tell some of their stories, which shocked Pops and made him start to understand a little of why they were still so nervous. They had had terrible experiences.

All Pops has now is one single photograph of those teenagers with their adopted mother. But God knows their stories intimately, everything is written down. Nothing of their suffering and bravery will be forgotten. Pops to his shame has forgotten many individual stories that have been told him through the years, but every story has been written down in heaven and in that day the books will be opened (Revelation Ch. 20 v.12) and every story read and judged. But happy are the ones whose names are found in that other book, the Book of Life; these are the ones who will see His face. What a Day that will be!

46
IT'S NOT TEA-TIME YET!

Pops is beginning to realise that his stories are like the fragments that remained after the feeding of the five thousand: they are not the main meal but what was left over after everyone had eaten and was full. All through the centuries, God has been doing wonderful and marvelous miracles for His children, mighty things that have changed the course of a nation's history, and sometimes, when Pops writes those things that he has seen God do for him, he feels that they are indeed just little fragments.

However, he was encouraged this morning when he read again John's account of the great miracle feast in chapter 6. When everyone was full, Jesus told his disciples to gather up the fragments so that nothing was lost. Then later on when Jesus warned the disciples of the hypocrisy of the religious rulers, likening it to bread that is puffed up, the disciples totally misunderstood what He was saying. They became worried because they had forgotten to bring bread with them and he had to remind them of the fragments left over from the great feast. So, even the fragments are important, and Pops doesn't want any of the things God has done for Nana, himself and his family and friends to be lost.

"The kids are going to be home from school and there is absolutely nothing in the house to feed them with, and I mean nothing! All I've got is a couple of pennies in my purse - what are we going to do, Dave?"

Pops had probably used the last of the money on a bag of cement because he was in the middle of making the meeting room bigger; now, with a brick in one hand and a trowel in the other, he shouts back to Nana, "It's not tea- time yet."

"Oh, ok," replies Nana (what a wife!) Ten minutes later there's a knock on the door, Nana goes to see who it is and there on the doorstep is a huge box of groceries, enough to satisfy the hunger of even the Oranges!

Many times after that, when there was no money or food Nana would say to herself, "It's not tea-time yet," and before the next meal was due God would have shown His hand providing in the most incredible ways. Maybe a twenty-pound note left on the fireplace, being treated to fish and chips, or someone putting a five- or ten-pound note in Pops's or Nana's pocket without them noticing, and it was always when it seemed there would be nothing for Nana to put on the table – and there were usually guests at the table too!

A friend of Pops, who had been a missionary in Kenya for many years, was speaking to a conference on the subject of believing prayer. In her teaching she was explaining how God can sometimes give us a vision or a dream to indicate how we should pray. She told how in a vision while she was praying, she saw a family sitting round the table but with no food on it and she described in detail the table, the family and the room. She took it that she must pray for God to provide for that family; while she was praying, she saw in the vision the kitchen door open and a hand appear putting loads of food on the table. She concluded that God had answered her prayer and thanked Him.

When she had finished speaking to the conference, a young

Russian woman came up to her and told her that the scene she described was the exact description of her family's kitchen, and that while her father was saying grace, although there was no food, a hand had opened the kitchen door just as she had described and covered the table with food. This is our Heavenly Father who gives us our daily bread.

Another friend of Pops, an evangelist, had been speaking all day to people on the street concerning their souls. He was on his way home, knowing however that there was nothing in his flat to eat and no money in his pocket. (Not all evangelists fly about in private jets.)

The Lord said to him, "Why not go and treat yourself to a meal in a restaurant?"

The evangelist said, "I've no money."

The Lord replied, "Here is a nice restaurant, go and sit down in there."

The evangelist, although a little nervous, obeyed. He sat down and then the Lord said, "Don't you say grace before a meal?" so with hands together and bowed head he thanked the Lord for what he was about to receive.

As soon as Pops's friend had finished praying, the restaurant owner came over to him and said he could have anything he liked off the menu!

"A long time ago," he said, "I vowed to God that if anyone came into my restaurant and said grace, I would give them the best meal I could produce. You are the first person to say grace in my restaurant, so what would you like to eat?"

Of all cheerful givers, God is the very best!

Jesus said, "Do not worry, your heavenly Father knows that you need all these things." Matthew Ch 6 v.25-34

47
HIDDEN TALENTS

Jena in East Germany is famous the world over for being the home of first-class optics, for binoculars, telescopes, microscopes and cameras, but even more famous in heaven for being the home of a dedicated bunch of Christians who made up His church all through the years of communism. When communism fell apart and the Berlin Wall came down, they were eager to tell their city all about their Lord and Saviour.

Friends of Pops, who had helped and supported the church in Jena for some time, asked Pops if he and his team could take the marquee and join them in an evangelistic mission. Pops said "Yes!" and so at Easter 1991 Pops and the team arrived in Jena.

Although West German goods were already pouring into East Germany, still the main transport in Jena were the Moskvitch and Wartburg cars and, of course, the cardboard box with the lawnmower engine: the world-famous Trabant!

But the big bully of the city roads was the electric tram. Nothing dare get in the way of the trams. They were the life blood of the city. Every road seemed to have them, and where there were trams then there were tram lines overhead and rails under your wheels. Under the wheels was not so big a problem, although Pops had to fight the steering wheel occasionally to get out of the rut of a tram rail; even a twenty-two-ton Mercedes truck with a bullbar should not argue with a determined East

German tram.

The scariest thing for Pops, though, was how low the overhead electrified tram lines were. The truck was about the highest vehicle on the road, and Pops didn't fancy him and the team getting fried by untamed East German electricity. Then right in the city centre the inevitable happened: the tram wires suddenly dipped to get under a main railway bridge in the city. Pops put the brakes on. There was only one thing to do:

"I need a volunteer to direct me under the wires," Pops shouted.

"I'll do it," shouted back Barry, and at that moment Barry became a legend in the annals of All for Jesus Missions. This was Barry's first mission with Pops. If it hadn't been, no doubt he would not have volunteered so readily, but would have taken the hint from the rest of the team who were pretending to be deep in prayer.

Fixed to the back of the truck, there was a ladder for climbing onto the roof to reach all the main beams of the marquee that were lashed down to special racks for transport. Pops told Barry to climb the ladder just far enough so he could see the top of the roof of the cab, the highest point on the truck, then with one hand to hold onto the ladder and with the other hand stretched out to wave Pops on if the tram wires were going to miss the truck: the signal Pops would watch out for in his mirror.

Pops firmly ignored the growing angry queue of trucks, Trabants and by now even a tram that had reluctantly stopped. When Barry was in place and had rehearsed his signals, Pops thanked the growing crowd of onlookers for all their expert advice.

He put the truck in gear and cautiously set off to the low bridge, keeping one eye on his mirror where he could see Barry's hand signalling to keep going. Twenty, ten, five metres - the truck was going to make it! Pops can still see Barry's hand waving him on.

At last, the truck was on the other side and the crowd started clapping. Pops shouted "Danke Schoen" or something like that, put his foot down and started to follow the directions he had been given to the mission site. Barry was now holding on for dear life and still signalling to Pops - but Pops was only thinking of how much time had been wasted negotiating electric wires and low bridges, and wanted to get to the site before it was too late to erect the marquee. He had completely forgotten about our hero Barry!

The first sight the brave German Christians had of their UK brethren was a massive truck speeding through their streets, weaving in and out of parked or abandoned Trabants, with a crazy Englishman hanging on to a ladder at the back, waving for all he was worth and shouting at the top of his voice, "Stop, stop!"

The German Christians greeted Pops and his flying circus with much love and grace, and never once asked themselves the inevitable question, "However did they win the war?"

Barry was a great hit with all the German Christians, especially the many young people who came to the meetings. He was a most remarkable linguist who spoke German perfectly, and Pops was told after a few days that he had even got hold of the local dialect. Pops also discovered that Barry had a Master's degree in Russian, which was a great help when they were confronted with angry border guards threatening them with AK47s.... but that's another story.

Barry could have chosen to have a high-flying career in languages but instead he chose to be a humble servant of Jesus, happy to have fellowship with those who preach the gospel.

Jesus said to his friend Peter, the big fisherman, over a meal of fish and bread: "Peter do you love Me more than these? Feed My sheep."

48
SUPPLY AND DEMAND

Pops understands there would be no stories worth writing if it were not for Jesus. Jesus is the story. His is the beginning and the end of the story. He is everything that happens in every chapter of every life that He comes into and commits Himself to.... and in the end the only life there will be is the life of Jesus.

All For Jesus Missions had been invited to Genoa to hold a tent mission. It would be the first time Pops would be preaching in Italy and he was excited. The team started making arrangements. The usual documents had to be made up.

In those days every country in Europe had their own borders and customs, which meant a truck travelling from Liverpool to Genoa would need paperwork from the customs at Liverpool docks to be presented at the customs at Dover, more papers presented at the border of France, then again from France to Italy. The Orange family's front room had become the mission's office, with an incredible full-time team, phoning, faxing, typing, talking to embassies etc. Pops was banned from the office. He was allowed to preach, put up tents, get through borders, speak to mayors and of course drive the truck - but it was a disaster to let him loose in the office.

The office had found a problem - in Italy all marquees must

have flame resistant material. The AFJM marquee, although up to UK regulations, would not be allowed into Italy. Pops needed a new tent!

Nana, after spending what seemed like hours on the telephone, discovered a company in Somerset who had just started to import a new type of marquee from France; they were calling it a barn marquee. It was totally fireproof and met all European regulations (which are a lot). So Nana and Pops decided to have day out and take a trip to Somerset.

The marquee company owned a very grand house and country estate. Pops drove down the long, beautiful drive and parked up his very old second-hand Saab next to the Jaguars and Rovers.

"It's a bit posh, Dave," says Nana.

"Don't worry! Just remember we have a Heavenly Father who is very rich," Pops says, wondering whether he has enough money to buy another couple of gallons of petrol to get home.

After coffee, sandwiches and biscuits (very posh sandwiches) they were shown round the marquees. Pops was impressed and decided on the biggest that could be erected without the use of a crane. Pops did fancy adding a crane to the mission's collection, but one look from Nana and Pops thought better of it. The cost of the marquee was £13,500 - a lot of money in the 1980s.

Back home the team was given the facts and then the team gave the facts to God.

"As usual, Lord, we haven't got any money! The marquee costs £13,500; we believe You want us to do this kind of evangelism; we promise we won't tell anyone or ask anyone for money except

You, Lord, because we want Your seal of approval and for people to see that You are the God who answers prayer. Thank You, Lord!"

Within a couple of weeks, a friend of Pops had decided to sell his business and wanted to give Pops £10,000 towards the marquee. The team was thrilled and believed God had said, "Yes go ahead," so Pops contacted the marquee people and ordered the brand new, all-singing, all-dancing marquee (the team did a bit of singing and dancing too).

Not long afterwards the Church in Genoa contacted Pops to say they had to cancel the tent mission. Pops was thrown and asked the Lord if He had got it wrong. The Lord kept quiet. Now, looking back, Pops can see the Lord was teaching him just to trust, but at the time things weren't so easy to understand or to explain to himself or to his friends. But within a week another letter arrived, this time from Portugal begging Pops to come back to Portugal for a whole summer of missions. God knows best how to direct his troops. All His troops have to do is trust and obey - and sometimes you end up with the bonus of a brand-new marquee!

Before travelling to Portugal, Pops had committed the new marquee to be used for the youth tent at a Christian Conference in sunny Devon, whilst the older canvas tent would be given to the conference to be used for missionary speakers. The marquee company had arranged to bring the marquee to the conference and show Pops how to erect it, and there was even a little video taken so Pops wouldn't forget how to do it.

After the marquee was up, Pops felt he had to tell the marquee people that straight after the conference had finished, he was committed to take the marquee to Portugal, but he realised that the rest of the cost of it had not as yet been paid. The marquee people said that was fine and he could pay the remaining £3,500 when he returned from Portugal. Pops had told the marquee people what it was being used for, and in his heart he wanted to show them that his God honours and pays in full all His promises, so he said to them, "When you come back at the end of the conference week to take the marquee down, I will have the rest of the money for you."

All through that week people were coming up to Pops congratulating him on the beautiful new marquee. Of course, they thought it was all bought and paid for, but Pops and Nana kept the secret of the £3,500 to themselves. Every morning that week Pops was expecting someone to say something like, "God has asked me to give you this," and hand over a cheque, but nobody did.

Saturday arrived and still no money. The marquee man was arriving at 10am. At 9.45am someone who Pops didn't know knocked on the door of the truck and asked, "How much do you need to pay for the marquee?" Pops was embarrassed to say how much it was, because to him it was a huge amount of money. The man got out his cheque book and insisted, "How much?"

Pops had to tell him and without a flicker the man made out a cheque for £3,500, by which time the marquee man had arrived and Pops's new very generous friend was able to hand the cheque over straight to the marquee man. Pops's new friend was very happy when he was told the full story; the marquee man was happy and surprised; Pops was happy because God was with him, and Pops believes God was very happy because He loves answering prayer!

49
JUST A TOOTHBRUSH

"We used to look over the river Prut to Romania and say, 'Those poor people: no food, no electricity, no lights anywhere.' Now it's the other way round. When we look over the river there are lights everywhere and it's us who have no electricity and no fuel."

Mikhail, a young Moldovan Pastor, was telling Pops how things had turned around. The dictator Ceausescu had been overthrown and Romania was now free from the clutches of Russia, no longer having to export the majority of their food to the east. However, communism in the USSR was now breaking up and as Moldova had no power of its own, they relied on Ukraine for their electricity. But Moldova had no money to pay Ukraine and Ukraine had stopped supplying electricity to them.

Mikhail and Pops were still talking as the young pastor showed Pops into his vegetable garden - no flowers because you can't eat flowers. The garden was impressive. There wasn't a foot wasted. Everywhere there were plants growing that would feed the pastor's family - and, as Pops was getting to know this wonderful young man, he suspected it would be feeding half the village too!

As Pops and Mikhail turned the corner of the house, Pops

was confronted with a scene he'd never thought he would see in Europe. There were the pastor's wife and his mother knee-deep in a hole filled with mud; they were cutting wheat stalks up with knives, throwing them into the mud and trampling them down with their feet. They were making bricks to repair their house after fierce storms had washed down most of the outside walls, which were also made with mud and straw bricks. There was no B&Q in Moldova; this was real Do It Yourself. But the whole family was praising and thanking God for the provision of mud and straw - that's when Pops fell in love with Moldova.

Mikhail and his wife lived in the south of the country. In the north, Pops discovered another remarkable family: Peter, his wife Ria and their children.

Peter owned a Kamaz, probably one of the best trucks ever built in Russia. Although northern Moldova was very fertile and had a good climate for growing all kinds of vegetables, because of the lack of money Peter's village (which we would call a small town) couldn't sell their produce. So Peter decided to load up his truck with the produce and drive north into the Arctic Circle (as you do!) to sell the villagers' produce to the workers on the oil drills and pipelines. With temperatures sometimes below -35 degrees these trips were very dangerous but if the villagers were to survive, this was the only way they could get a decent price for all their hard work.

On one of the visits to Peter's village it was arranged for the team to visit and preach in a number of prisons. The last prison the team visited was about a two-hour journey from Peter's home. All the team were up early, keen to be the first to use the outside toilet - "the facilities" as Jo called it. This consisted of a tin bowl: when it was full, the contents were thrown onto the soil where the vegetables would be planted. Ria grew wonderful-looking vegetables!

When it was Pops's turn for the "facilities" he had to pass through the yard, where he discovered Peter had taken the whole engine and gearbox out of his beloved Lada and spread it over most of the front yard.

"Don't worry, it will be all done before breakfast," smiled Peter. "Stalin machines always need repairing."

Time to leave for the prison and sure enough the 'Stalin machine' was ticking over just beautifully. On the road Pops wondered why Peter kept his arm out of the car window.

"This accelerator," explained Peter. Around his hand he had tied a piece of string which then disappeared under the bonnet: the other end was tied to the carburettor, which explained why there was a hole where the accelerator pedal should be!

"Automatique!" Peter proudly explained.

At the prison the team sang some songs and explained how they had been saved, and Pops preached. When possible, Pops liked to take clothes, shoes, and toiletries into the prisons to give to the prisoners, but as this was the last place to be visited, there was hardly anything left; by the time the last prisoner appeared all that Pops had left was one toothbrush. He didn't know what do. Would it be an insult just to give a toothbrush? The prisoner was a young woman, maybe in her early twenties. She held out her hands and as Pops gave her the toothbrush, tears filled her eyes. She took it as if it had been a diamond ring, held it close to her and kissed Pops's hand. Pops looked at the prison captain, who said, "She's been asking for a toothbrush for months, but we have none to give her." Pops had nothing to give this young woman but a toothbrush, and a toothbrush was all she wanted.

Our government has just spent close to £300bn helping us tackle the pandemic - that's a lot of toothbrushes! At the judgement, Jesus will call the nations to stand before his throne and judge us on how we have looked out for one another. (Matthew Ch. 25 v.31-46)

50
JUST SAY "YES"

Pops was helping the 'Happy Church' (a great name for a church, Pops thought) with a preaching crusade in Nakuru, Kenya, very close to Nakuru Lake and nature reserve, the home of thousands of flamingos, huge water buffalo and the odd leopard. He was staying with a couple who were part of the leadership in the church. They were on fire for God. The church had bought the local cinema and it was filled with over a thousand in the congregation.

God was pouring out His wonderful Spirit and many healings were taking place. Because of that, Pops was eager to know how things had started and how the new friends he was staying with had become Christians. So, over the evening meal Pops asked Robert, the husband, to tell him his story, expecting to be amazed and thrilled with what he was about to hear.

"Well," said Robert, "A missionary came to our school when I was a young teenager, told the gospel to us all and then said, 'If anyone wants to be saved and know Jesus with all your heart, just say 'YES' to Jesus and put your hand up.'

"I wanted Jesus and prayed YES in my heart and put my hand up and God just came there and then, filled me with His Spirit, and I fell in love with Jesus."

"That's it?" said Pops, "As simple as that?"

"Yes, as simple as that, and God has put fire in my heart ever since."

The Pod People met each other on the mission in Jena, East Germany, and within eighteen months they were married and settled down to married life in Bournemouth. Up in Liverpool, Nana was beginning to worry about how much driving Pops was doing. There were more and more opportunities for missions and all the time Eastern Europe was opening up, which meant a lot more driving time.

"You need someone to help with driving the truck, Dave," Nana said one day. Pops looked at her, but Nana could read his mind.

"No, not me!" she said. "You need a man with his own HGV licence."

Pops didn't like to admit it, but he knew as usual Nana was right. After a few days struggling with the thought of someone else driving his beloved truck, Pops gave in and said, "Ok, Pen, you're right, we will pray."

Back in Bournemouth God had started to speak to the Pod People about leaving Bournemouth for Liverpool and helping All for Jesus Missions. They contacted Pops and told him what they believed the Lord might be saying.

"Brilliant!" said Pops. "Can you drive a truck?"

"Not yet, but I could if I take my HGV test."

The Pod People would have a great deal to give up, leaving friends, their church and their home, and giving up their jobs in order to join Nana and Pops in Liverpool. Nana would be great to work with, but Pops? Some people said he was a bit, well, 'Pops'.

The Pod People (Dave & Liz) prayed some more and believed God said, "Go" and so they simply said "YES" and joined AFJM. Liz became an incredible organiser on missions, and when Nana wasn't travelling Liz took on the role of bullying Pops to be in the right place at the right time. And later on, she was Nana's 'right arm' with opening and running Gladstone's Christian Coffee Bar. Dave got his HGV licence and, among his many other talents, drove the truck all over Europe with Pops's blessing.

Oh, and the reason they were called the Pod People is because they were the only married couple who could get into the pod above the truck's cab to sleep; they were very fit!

In the early days back in Leamington, Pops seemed to be always preaching about the baptism in the Holy Spirit, how God wanted to fill his children with Himself and His love.

One afternoon a friend of Nana and Pops came to talk to him. She looked troubled and close to tears, so Pops sat her down and Nana put the kettle on.

"What's the matter?" asked Pops.

Between sobs Selina said, "I want to be filled with Jesus' Spirit. I've asked and asked but nothing's happened."

"OK," said Pops, "Let's see what Jesus says."

They both opened the Bible and looked at the conversation that Jesus had with His beloved disciples in the upper room, when He was talking about the Comforter, the Holy Spirit, who Jesus said would be sent from the Father to all that believe in Jesus.

See John chapter 15 v.24: "Ask and you will receive that your joy may be full."

"Well," said Pops to Selina, "Have you asked?"

"Yes," said Selina.

"Have you received?" Pops asked.

"No," said Selina.

Pops again said, "But you have asked Jesus and Jesus has promised that all that ask will receive. 'God is not a man that He should lie,' so have you received?"

She still looked a little confused.

Pops said, "If I give you a gift, what do you do?"

"I receive it."

"Well," Pops said, "Jesus is giving you a gift, so what do you do?"

"I receive it!" Slowly, light began to pour into her heart. "Yes, of course, He's come, I've received!"

Selina's face lit up with the glory of God; Pops will never

forget it, the whole room seemed filled with His presence.

Whenever Nana and Pops meet Selina that same glory is on her face, the glory that comes with always saying "YES" to Jesus and His promises.

51
WHAT'S NEXT?

For a long time Nana and Pops have wanted to write down some of the wonderful things that God has done for them. It would be done mainly for their grandchildren but also for anyone else who might be interested.

They wanted to show that if God was willing to be gracious to the likes of Nana and Pops (especially Pops who, if you have read the stories from the beginning, you will know deserves nothing of God's kindness, who was an angry young man with a big chip on his shoulder and foolishness in his heart), then He wants to be gracious to all, and is ready to pour out His love and goodness to anyone who seeks after Him.

A year ago this week (1st year of lock down, 2020) Pops believed that the Lord put it in his heart to write down these little stories, and every Thursday and Friday since then He has brought something to mind that Pops could write about - which is a miracle in itself.

If, after reading the stories, any of you have spotted mistakes, please let Nana know. In the case of Pops's animal stories, Pops is sure penguins and their fellow creatures have a mind of their own, but he doesn't profess to be able to read them.

Nana has just started to record the stories and with the help of Daniel (Number 1 son) they will be going on YouTube. (Editor's note by Dan: they're all now uploaded.) www.daveandpennyorange.squarespace.com

Pops believes, hopes, and prays that his children and their children will experience a thousand times more miracles than Pops and Nana have seen, and that God would give them great big hearts and a huge hunger to know the 'width and length and depth and height of the love of Jesus.'

On the telly people have got very excited about bits of stuff that have travelled all the way from earth and have landed on Mars, now sending information back to man about the red planet. Dedicated scientists, engineers and mathematicians must have spent hundreds of hours and denied themselves so much to achieve their goal but, oh, who will do the same to explore God, to "experience the depths of Jesus Christ"?

If eventually men do get to live on Mars, one thing that will be sure is that they will take sin with them; that will be inevitable and the problems that we have on earth will be the same problems on Mars. But if our young people (the next generation) explore God and by a new birth live in His kingdom, then the treasures they will discover are too numerous to count: righteousness, holiness, love, power, joy, faith and their great reward, God Himself.

Children, grandchildren, friends: hunger, thirst, pray harder, pray longer, pray louder, and you will see things that Pops hasn't even dreamt of.

Pops knows he has been a very poor example of what a Christian ought to be, but if God was willing to do something with him, think what He wants to do with you. There are thousands of Pops's contemporaries who have done and seen far greater things than Pops; all of them can witness to God's everlasting faithfulness.

Then there are those mighty ones who have gone before, people like George Fox, George Whitfield, Madam Guyon, George Muller, Helen Roseveare, Hudson Taylor, Corrie Ten Boom, Amy Carmichael, Rees Howells, John Lake, Mildred Cable, Gladys Aylward, Richard Wurmbrand, Dr Martyn Lloyd-Jones, David Wilkerson, Charles Finney, Duncan Campbell, William Seymour, D.L. Moody, David Brainerd, C.T. Studd, William Booth, Catherine Booth, the Marechale, and many more.

You don't have to agree with everything they said but if you walk with them, you are sure to catch some of their fire. All have been shining lights and have helped Pops in his walk with God. Get to know these pioneers for God and let their lives speak to you.

Let's all keep 'looking unto Jesus' and as we hear Him say, "Take up your cross and follow Me," by the grace of God we will be able to say, "Yes, Lord, with all our hearts."

"And they who love God cannot love Him by measure.

For their love is but hunger to love Him still better"

- Frederick William Faber

52
EXTRA, EXTRA, READ ALL ABOUT IT...

Pops wasn't around for this last story but he reckons it might have gone something like this.

"He's alive, he's alive, can't anybody hear me? He's alive! Peter, John, James, anybody? He's alive!" She keeps on shouting and banging on the door.

The door opens, slowly, cautiously, but she can't be doing with slowly, so with two hands and then her shoulder pushing as hard against the door as she can, she bursts in. The disciples jump up, back away from her, frightened, and then bewildered and then curious.

"It's Jesus - I've seen Him, He's alive, He spoke to me!"

Peter's jaw drops, he tries to speak - it takes a lot for Peter to be lost for words!

"Mary, you saw Him? But... but... He's dead, they crucified Him. Mary, He's been dead and buried for three days."

John puts his hand gently on Mary's arm and asks, "What did He say to you?"

"He spoke my name, He said 'Mary' and I knew it was Him."

Peter and John look at each other and like all good mates they know what each other is thinking. Immediately they head for the door, tumble down the stairs and out onto the street. The garden, where the tomb is, is some distance away, but they run as fast as they can anyway.

John gets there first; the big stone in front of the tomb has somehow been rolled away - he stops at the entrance, not knowing what he should do. Peter gets there panting; he goes straight in - there is no body, just the cloth that was wrapped around Jesus and the face cloth folded neatly by itself. John follows his friend into the tomb, sees it is empty and he believes.

"Peter, this is what the Lord said, after three days He would rise from the dead.

He has risen!"

"Yes, yes, you're right - we must tell everyone! Come on, John, back to the rest of the disciples!"

"It's true, it's true, Mary is right. He has risen from the dead - everything He said, it's true."

Everybody starts talking at once, well, more like shouting, with some believing, some still doubting. Suddenly Jesus appears in the centre of them all.

"Peace to you."

Still some can't quite believe it is really the Lord.

Jesus says, "Look at my hands and feet."

They look and see the holes where the soldiers had nailed Him to the cross, they touch Him and know it isn't a dream but Jesus Himself.

****

In the next few weeks over five hundred people saw Him indifferent places at different times, until the day came when He was taken up to heaven.

Before He went, Jesus said, "Go into all the world and preach this good news to every creature and know I AM with you always."

This is the best story ever! Jesus was crucified, dead and buried, and on the third day He rose from the dead and now is alive for evermore. He gives life to everyone who asks and those who receive Him will live with Him forever.

Printed in Great Britain
by Amazon